The Broker Who Broke Free

The Broker Who Broke Free

By

Oliver Seligman

Other books by Oliver Seligman

Befriending Bipolar: a patient's perspective

CONTENTS

For the heroes who are willing to do whatever it takes to be free.

This is a true story.

Prologue

What am I doing with my life?

"The thing with money is, it makes you do the things you don't want to do."

– Lou Mannheim, character in Wall Street.

A top investment bank, London. 8 a.m. November 2000.

It is Monday morning. My eyes are sunk into dark sockets, my skin is clammy and I have far too many wrinkles. I feel trapped, like a fox in a hole. A pack of hounds above me, baying for my blood. A tight knot sits in my stomach and troubled thoughts bounce around my head. It has been two hours since I arrived at work, two hours spent thinking about how much I hate my life. It is so hard to be present.

Six flat screen TVs stand in front of me, with

hundreds of share prices flashing and changing every second. Over three hundred names, trading codes, highs and lows, bids and sells, as well as the volumes traded that day. Numbers, numbers, numbers and somehow, I need to keep track of them. Any oversight, any mistake, any missed trade or overzealous bid and the phone rings. If my client is having a good day, he will be irritated by my mistake. If he is having a bad day, the four-letter words will fly, along with the kitchen sink.

Two heavy, black plastic phones lie to the left and right of my desk, waiting for my next client to ring. On quiet days I use only the phone on the right. When the market heats up, both are tucked under under my chin, as I scramble to scribble orders coming in like sushi dishes on a conveyor belt. As I stare at their tangled chords, I am reminded of yesterday's final trade. A trade where I had a screaming match with a client whose heart had been sealed shut with molten lead. My life is not what I had hoped it would be. It has become one long hangover.

Back then I knew there must be more to life, but what it was remained a mystery to me. I was making a small fortune, but I didn't enjoy the good things anymore. I was existing rather than living.

"What the hell am I doing with my life?"

I asked myself, day after day. Yet still I did it. Still, I turned up for work, an unseen force pushing me to sell my soul as a sales trader in one of the hottest financial cauldrons on earth. To those who knew me it didn't make much sense. Where had the fun-loving, Ollie gone? Why was he working as a Sales Trader in an investment back when he had the mathematical acumen of a cane toad?

"Just keep going, only one more year, that's all."

I told myself, but keeping going hurt. Perhaps it was ambition? Perhaps it was fear? Perhaps I had no idea how else I could make so much money?

Whatever was pushing me, led me to live a life that didn't suit me. A life I didn't want. I was chasing the dream of financial freedom. Yes, I was chasing the "dream," but forgetting to enjoy life along the way. I was twenty-five years old, but felt like an old man, aching with a boredom which filled my so-called "successful" life.

Strangely, my unhappiness had less to do with my job than I appreciated back then. If I could have taken a step back, I might have seen that sales trading wasn't as bad as I thought. After all, I was working in one of the most exciting places on earth, right in the heart of the City of London, the centre of the financial world. A risky, lively place, where fortunes could be made or lost in minutes. The riches, the bonuses, the fast cars, the luxury holidays and admiring looks, were marching closer every year. I was moving swiftly towards my goal and if I kept my nose to the grindstone, I would have it all.

Some of my colleagues loved their job. The prestige of working on the trading floor swelled their pride and their bank balances didn't do too badly either. But this didn't help me. My problem was my mind. My head was cluttered with an endless dialogue, pulling me in different directions, ruining my fun and stressing my mind towards breaking point.

"*Quit.*"
"*Don't quit.*"
"*The money's too good — just hang in there for a few more years.*"
"*Nothing's worth this pain.*"

Chatter, chatter, chatter. The voices in my head waged a relentless internal tug of war, which began at sunrise and only abated after a few drinks in one of the wine bars in St. Paul's. I wasn't cut out for this level of stress.

I spent those years in finance entangled in my mind, living my life in a cage between my ears. I was a prisoner in the most maximum of maximum security prisons and the reason I couldn't escape? I didn't know the prison existed.

I thought I could do anything if the cash was good enough, but life was proving me wrong. I was clinging onto the money and the possibilities it gave, but at the same time living in this prison of my own creation.

The longer I hung in there, the lower my mood sank and the tougher life became. I was so self-consumed I didn't see what was staring me in the face; I needed to give up chasing the dollar, discover my life's purpose and follow that. Instead, I kept trudging the wrong way up a painful path, hoping someone would save me, oblivious to the fact that it was up to me to save myself.

That was over two decades ago and now my life and my mind are rather different. In truth, they are unrecognisable. I was hesitant to tell my story, but fate led me from the trading floor, through a series of adventures and I emerged with a tale to tell. A tale which might inspire or entertain you. This book is short because writing about peace is nothing compared to experiencing it for yourself. Its purpose is to highlight the little-known fact; that it is possible to free oneself from the slavery of the mind — to move beyond stresses, worries and emotional suffering and to find peace with oneself and the world. Cultivating a state of inner presence, not unlike the state that small children experience much of the time, is achievable. Some call this state Nirvana, others Samadhi. I like to call it true happiness or peace. The name is not important, finding it is.

Chapter 1. Earning a crust

"If you do what you love, you'll never work a day in your life."

– Marc Anthony, musician

Seven years before my foray into the financial world, I had been struck down by an illness of the mind. As a far from fully grown seventeen-year-old, I found myself an inpatient in a mental hospital in Edinburgh experiencing the darkest depths of depression. I couldn't eat, I could barely speak and to make matters worse, each moment felt like hell and seemed to last forever. Later that year, a psychiatrist diagnosed me with manic depression or bipolar disorder as it is now known.

After a year and a half of trying to live a normal life but failing miserably, I was put on a psychiatric drug called lithium. Lithium controlled the worst of the euphoric highs and debilitating lows of bipolar, but the medication had its downsides too. The side effects were tough and my once vibrant emotional life vanished as the dampening effects of the drug stole my feelings away. However, the upside was worth it. Taking lithium enabled me to function again. I could now begin to rebuild the life I had left behind. No longer tormented by ghastly depressions, destructive manias, or terrifying psychoses, I went to Newcastle University and rejoined my peers in search of a happy and successful life.

I graduated from university with a degree in Zoology and no intention of ever working with animals. After three years of peering at the poor blighters down a microscope and cutting them into little pieces, I had had enough. I got a job building horse jumps in the Highlands of Scotland, which could be classed as working with animals, but I didn't sit on a horse once and only patted them occasionally. Horses made me very nervous.

It was a terrific job. I worked with some great people and I loved being outdoors. We used whatever we could lay our hands on to build magnificent jumps, which professional event riders leapt over on their trusty steeds. I spent my days using chainsaws, hammering nails, driving trucks and eating junk food, and my nights living in a smelly old caravan which should have been condemned. Bipolar seemed a thing of the past and my job was pretty much heaven on earth for a young guy with no responsibilities.

I travelled around Britain doing work which

satisfied me, surrounded by friends, going to parties and having a high old time. Some days I lived in the smelly, old caravan and others I slept in the wings of stately homes, so vast I could have got lost in them. They say variety is the spice of life and in those joyful days I got plenty of it.

Many of the riders I met were inspirational. Galloping across the countryside, they threw themselves and their huge beasts over jumps which might kill lesser riders. I was in awe of them. Whenever they entered a competition, they never knew if they were going to make it home in one piece! Yet still they rode on and usually with a smile on their face. Here were people who lived for the moment. They were friendly, fun, generous and brave and being around them was a privilege. To this day, that simple, menial, low paid work was one of the most enjoyable jobs I have had, but back then I wasn't easily satisfied. My mind was restless and ambitious, always on the lookout for better things to do or other goals to achieve.

Since I was small, I had a sense there was something significant I was meant to do with my life. I believed I had been born with a purpose to fulfill, but what that purpose was had evaded me. Have you ever felt like that? That there is something important you are meant to do, but you don't know what it is?

One morning, I woke up in the cramped confines of the caravan. It smelt worse than ever. The windows were fogged up and covered in a thick, green mould that seemed to have crept closer during the night, like an alien fungus from a bad B movie. Although I was famished, I didn't dare to open the fridge for fear of what might be living in it. It was winter in the north of Scotland; the electric heater was broken and I was bloody freezing.

I had been thinking about my future for a few weeks. Yes, I liked the freedom of building jumps, but as far as I was concerned, it wasn't a job for someone who wanted to make an impact in life. I needed to get myself a proper career, with prestige, prospects and money. A job people would admire and respect me for. The clock was ticking and I couldn't waste my time having fun forever.

Lying in bed, breathing in the caravan's stuffy air, I began to dream up a cunning plan. If I became an equities broker, or trader as the Americans called it, I could make an outrageous amount of money in a decade or so. If I invested this money wisely, within ten years I would be able to buy a house on the beach in Thailand. I had never been to Thailand, but I knew I would have the sun, the white sand, the tropical rainforest and not a care in the world. I could live there, do some consulting work and live off my investments. Who wouldn't be happy living on the beach in a tropical paradise?

That day I quit my job.

Chapter 2. Dick Whittington

"Money often costs too much."

– Ralph Waldo Emerson, philosopher & lecturer

A few weeks later, I packed a bag and moved to London. Being out of the caravan was a relief and although I missed my friends, the time had come for me to embark upon a new adventure and make some serious cash.

It was the nineties and at that time the global economy was booming. So, it didn't take me long to get a temping job settling trades in the "back office" of an American bank in the Docklands. My first temping job was in Canary Wharf and was far from glamorous. In those days, Canary Wharf and the Docklands were relatively new developments and to call the area sterile would have been paying it a great compliment. All steel and concrete, with little charm, Canary Wharf felt like a cross between a graveyard and a doctor's waiting room.

On my first day at work, my footsteps echoed on the hard, polished floor of the arrival hall at Canary Wharf Tube station. The smell of metal and heavy-duty paint filled my nostrils, as I stopped to stare at what looked like an aircraft hangar, but was in fact the lower level of a Tube station. After taking the elevator upwards, I emerged into the dull, grey mist of a February morning and shuddered. The sheer number of lost souls marching to and fro, going about their business with perma-frowns on their pale faces shocked me. These poor people, beaten down by the brutally long workdays they chose to endure, were the polar opposite of the event riders I so admired.

"That's not going to happen to me," I told myself overconfidently, *"Not me."*

The excitement of the job matched the charm of the area. At first, I didn't mind, as settling trades was a foot in the door and a formidable boost to my CV. However, as the weeks went by the back office turned out to be more tedious than I could have imagined. I basically worked as a human computer, double checking numbers and settling trades. Sitting at my desk for hours on end, I pretended to be busy when I wasn't. What made it worse was the fact that I was devoid of mathematical talent. Maths had been my weakest subject at school and here I was working as a number cruncher in a bank.

At that time, the American work ethic was storming the walls of the City of London. It was simple; work hard and then work some more and if your boss thinks you're lazy you're not going to last long. So, against my better instincts I planted my bottom on my chair and remained there all day. At a time when Facebook was no more than a glint in Mark Zuckerberg's eye, there was little to distract me from the boredom. If I didn't have any work to do, rather than grab a coffee and have a chat with a colleague, I was compelled to stay at my desk and look busy. As you can imagine, a large portion of my day consisted of daydreaming as I hunched over my computer pretending to work. It was all about pretending — pretending to work, pretending I was interested, pretending everything was okay. I began to miss my caravan.

Luckily at school, I had mastered the little-known technique of "nodding with a serious expression on my face," whenever I was presented with a boring situation. If a geography teacher talked to me about the glacial formation of truncated spurs or lectured me on why out of town supermarkets were the death of local butchers, I looked them in the eye, furrowed my brow and nodded sincerely. Often, I didn't even hear what they were saying, but it seemed to keep them happy. This nodding technique proved as invaluable in the bank as it had been at school and after a few months there was even talk of a promotion.

I wasn't keen to take on another boring back-office job, I had bigger fish to fry. All the trades I settled came from the mysterious "front office," more commonly known as the trading floor. As far as I was concerned the trading floor was the Holy Grail; a chaotic, dangerous place where billions of dollars were thrown around and fortunes were made and lost between heartbeats. Here was where equity in the world's biggest and most powerful companies was traded by the richest organisations in the world. I didn't want to settle the front office's trades. I wanted to be the one making them.

Although I had never met one in the flesh, I had watched Wall Street and was convinced the equities traders were the real men around town. They were the ones who got the hottest women and drove the fastest cars. They wore Armani suits, Patek Philippe watches, Church shoes and drove top of the range Porches and Ferraris. Money was no object to these larger-than-life characters. Confident and impressive, they lived life on the edge. Like lions they ruled the jungle and everyone knew it.

I also humbly knew I had it in me to be the best sales trader who had ever walked the earth. I would be one of those lions. It was my destiny. Growl. Yes, I was a lion…

This slightly deluded pussycat didn't realise he was in for a nasty surprise.

I chuckle when I look at how I thought the

world worked back then. At school, I had been taught that if I got good grades I would get into a good university. If I left a good university with a good degree, I would get a good job, preferably a well-paid one. If I did well at work and got promoted, I could buy fancy cars, go on expensive holidays, find a beautiful wife and send my children to the same expensive boarding school I had been sent to. Here they could learn the same thing and repeat it over again.

I wasn't alone in clinging onto these ideas. Ideas which told me that happiness lay in the letters after my name or the number of zeroes in my bank balance. I was never encouraged to find out what I really enjoyed doing and pursue a career in that. The wheel of academia was the main focus and getting the grades to get me to the top. Although this strategy is commonly taught, it has one fundamental downside. It rarely works.

After a brain numbingly dull year in the back office, I had worked for long enough to convince any future employer that I had an undying commitment to capitalism and was willing to put myself through hell on earth to be rich; two traits held in high regard on the trading floor. Now the time to muscle my way into the lion's den had arrived.

Interviewing for positions in the most powerful investment banks on earth was a rush. I loved it. Whenever I donned my pinstriped suit, straightened my tie and pushed my way through the glass doors of some deliriously wealthy financial institution, I felt indestructible. Stepping into a world where only the few dared to tread stroked my ego and made me feel very special indeed.

The traders who interviewed me were impressive, driven and intent on discovering what I was made of. I loved the feeling of importance that filled me whenever I entered their domain. I was moving into the realm of the movers and shakers, where the people who made things happen prowled. Here were the ones who had real power, perhaps even more power than the politicians; because they controlled the money and didn't have to answer to voters. If I played my cards right, I would get a whiff of that power.

Back then, those interviews meant I was becoming "somebody." I mattered, or so I thought. They were like a drug to me and I made sure I got my fix.

The interviews themselves were something of an enigma. I was never completely sure what they were looking for, but I figured that schmoozing the interviewer without being caught schmoozing was the way to go. Maintaining the fine balance between saying the right thing and not looking like an arse-kisser was a talent I prided myself in. A talent that once again I can attribute to my school days.

"What are your weaknesses?" some Maserati-driving big shot asked me.

"I'm a perfectionist and I tend to work too hard," I replied with a furrowed brow, once again using the nodding technique to great effect.

Or I might say, "Sometimes I give it everything and get exhausted. That's my biggest weakness."

They must have heard these corny lines a hundred times, but perhaps they recognised that, with the right training, this cocky young man could make them money. I guess that was what the interviews were all about: working out if the candidate could make money for the bank and, more importantly, boost the interviewer's own bonuses.

In these interviews my ethics, morals and beliefs were irrelevant. No one asked me if I felt that honesty or integrity were important, and in those days I didn't spent much time thinking about either. Investment banks were no place for do-gooders or bleeding hearts — it was the City of London. People were only useful when they were making money.

The nodding technique worked its magic and I was offered places on some fast-track Graduate Training Programmes in half a dozen banks. One stood out, because it included a six and a half thousand-pound bonus just for taking the job and a two-month, all-expenses-paid training course in New York.

Dazzled by this new world, I was sucked into the lure of big money and soon forgot about the things which had meant a great deal to me: helping people, having fun and making the world a better place. The new me cared far more about my pay cheque than my happiness. Or rather, the new me thought my paycheck would bring me happiness. So, with dollar bills in my eyes, I signed on the dotted line and was enrolled as a sales trader in one of the biggest financial machines on earth.

Chapter 3. The Big Apple

"Pride comes before a fall."

– Ancient proverb

Standing in the lobby of the biggest, multi-national, banking juggernaut in existence, was awe inspiring. Everything about this place hummed with affluence. The grey-white walls were built from of solid marble, the doors seamed with polished bronze and even the lifts sang soothing sounds when they arrived at your floor. I had been summoned to my new employer's Head Office, to fill out some paperwork before I was allowed to begin working on the trading floor. A few weeks working in the London office and then I would be flown to New York to take a big bite out of the Big Apple. To say I was pleased with myself would have been an understatement. I had arrived. It was my time.

After I had signed the paperwork, a striking good-looking receptionist handed me an identity badge and my smile broadened. Finally, my quest for financial freedom was underway. I was about to embark on an adventure which would give me all the things a young man with no clue about life thinks matter: fast cars, fancy houses and sex appeal.

My material dreams were closer to fulfillment than ever, but my brazen confidence hid a steel trap that lay in wait for me, set by dark forces deep in my unconscious. I felt I had put bipolar behind me, but within a few months of living in London my head went array once more.

It all began late one Saturday afternoon whilst travelling into London on the Underground. As the doors closed and the train pulled out of Turnpike Lane, I caught a whiff of burning plastic. My stomach tightened. The Underground was the last place on earth I would ever want to smell anything burning. Fear welled up inside me, my mouth went dry and my heart began to thump. I looked to my right and left, to see if the other passengers had smelt the burning. Their "rabbit in the headlights" expressions told me I was not imagining it.

Before I could do anything, the doors sealed shut and the train pulled away. I held my breath, hoping if I couldn't smell the burning it might go away. At the next station the acrid smell was unmistakable.

"Oh, bollocks," I thought. *"Should I get off?"*

I could see the other passengers thinking the same thing, but again the doors closed and the train accelerated away. A crackling sound came over the intercom, but the distorted Cockney voice which invariably followed, remained silent.

"Has the fire burned the intercom? Am I about to be burned alive?"

A few nerve-wracking minutes later, the doors opened at Finsbury Park. The smell of smoke was gone.

"Thank goodness."

I bolted off the train and sprinted up the escalators as fast as I could. Hurdling the barriers, I spied the exit and jogged to a walk. Leaving the station, I smiled. London air had never smelled so good.

That evening, in the safety of my flat, I poured myself a whiskey, but my trembling hand spilled most of it on the kitchen counter.

The following week, I was waiting for a train at Fulham Broadway when a stifling sense of fear hit me out of nowhere. My head spinning, I stepped back and leant one hand against a wall to steady myself. The dizziness continued and was joined by an abject sense of terror moving upwards through my body. I had no idea what to do. So, I fought the feeling as best as I could. The more I fought it the more intense it became.

After what felt like an age but was more like a minute, the fear subsided. Looking around the platform, I could see that none of the other passengers had noticed my mini meltdown. In one way this was a relief, but in another I felt terribly lonely. I wanted a hug, but instead I was left leaning against a cold, concrete wall puffing and panting as quietly as I could. This was the beginning of an unpleasant relationship with panic attacks which was to last for a few years.

Soon afterwards, I had another attack. This time in the commuter filled chaos of rush hour, when I was pressed up against a group of stressed-out suits in a crowded carriage. Was this going to become a regular thing?

The panic attacks were horrible, but worse was worrying about when the next one would strike. The fear of the next attack wasn't as acute as the attacks themselves, but sat in the back of my mind, knowing away at me as I went about my business. It didn't occur to me that the attacks had anything to do with bipolar and I didn't think about going to a doctor to get some advice. I just crossed my fingers and got on with my new London life.

After two months of sitting next to sales traders in the London office, slowly learning what it took to be a success in the City, it was time for me to fly to America. My employers put me up in the Lexington hotel on Lexington Avenue in

Manhattan Island, not far from the Chrysler Building. The Lexington was built on some of the world's most expensive real estate and my room was luxurious. I had an enormous, flat screened television at the end of my bed and an en-suite bathroom nearly as large as the room itself. The breakfasts were first class and the room service top notch. I could order a top class, medium rare steak to my room and be feasting on it minutes later. Here I was being educated in the ways of equities trading, whilst living like a king only a minute's walk from the world famous Chrysler Building. I was learning how to be a Gordon Gekko, right in the heart of New York and I was getting paid for it!

Had I been older and wiser, I would have known that in the cut-throat world of high finance, no one gets something for nothing. But this thought never crossed my mind. I lived it up, being wined and dined in fine restaurants and hanging out in trendy bars in wealthy districts of the US capital. Tasting the high life and the opulence that came with working for an investment bank was addictive. There was something too appealing about being someone important, someone who had enough money to enjoy the finer things in life and not worry about the consequences.

Another highlight of living in the Big Apple were the breakfasts. Every Saturday and Sunday, our gang of banking graduates went for breakfast at a local diner across the road from the Lexington hotel. The variety of food on offer was staggering.

Short stack waffles, full stack waffles, old-fashioned waffles, Belgian waffles or waffles on the side. I was used to British breakfast menus which were a couple of paragraphs long, but in New York the menus were Biblical. Even with the most efficient of waitresses, it took us ten minutes to order and over an hour to eat.

New York life wasn't all fun and games. We did have some work to do. The graduates on the Graduate Training Program were not fully integrated into the bank, so we had our own office area where we studied and took exams. In the first week of my training, a stern looking banker with a Mississippi drawl, handed all of us a thick blue folder with the words:

"Series 7 General Securities Representative Exam" emblazoned on the front in intimidating black letters. I flicked through the folder, which contained a massive amount of information on securities, stocks, shares, bonds and other financial instruments and regulations.

"Not exactly light reading," I commented to the woman sitting next to me.

She giggled.

"You got that," the man from Mississippi replied with a hint of irritation in his voice. I was later to learn that he had made it to a senior position the hard way. Leaving school at fifteen and getting a job as a delivery boy in the bank. He had worked his way up from the mail room and didn't seem too excited about being in charge of the group of privileged graduates sitting in front of him.

"Whoops," I whispered. This time out of earshot.

"This little beauty is your light reading for the next six weeks," he told us sarcastically, holding up the folder for all to see. "You need to learn everything in it. You got to know it back to front and inside out. I want you dreaming the answers in your sleep."

"He thinks he's the drill sergeant from An Officer and a Gentleman," I whispered.

The woman laughed.

"Six weeks?" someone thought out loud.

"Yup, you kids got to learn it in your free time. We aren't wasting no class time on this."

"What's the pass mark?"

"Seventy percent and you don't get a second chance. If you fail, go get another job," he declared, then added with a hint of bitterness,

"I'm sure a bunch of Ivy League geniuses like you'll be fine."

I hoped so, because if I failed this multiple-choice nightmare, my dream would be over only weeks after it had begun.

To describe the information in the blue file as bland would have been generous. Then again, the Series 7 was not designed to excite. It was designed to make sure that aspiring sales traders such didn't do a Nick Leeson and bankrupt one of the most prestigious banks in the world.

The liveliness of New York was invigorating and I vowed to make the most of my time whilst I was there; walking the city streets, visiting museums, shops and spending time in Greenwich Park. There were about thirty students on the Graduate Training Programme, most of whom came from top universities such as Harvard, Yale, Oxford, Cambridge and the London School of Economics.

Graham, one of my closest colleagues, was a particularly bright man. He had graduated from Cambridge with a first-class degree in astrophysics and possessed a photographic memory. He was different to many of the other graduates because he had a dream beyond making more money than he would ever need. His dream was to build a rocket ship to propel him into outer space.

"When I make it as a derivatives trader, I'm going to build a rocket and become the first man to reach the stratosphere without government funding," he told me in a matter-of-fact way, one day whilst we were eating lunch. I enjoyed talking to Graham about his dream because he was so enthusiastic about it. Enthusiastic people can talk about almost anything and I find them interesting. Graham was determined to be different and I could relate to this. To this day, I still hope to read about his successful trip into outer space and see him smiling through a porthole, ten thousand metres above sea level.

From time to time, experienced traders would come and lecture us on different topics. These lectures, like the traders themselves, were intelligent and entertaining, filled with insight, dark humour and tips on how to ruthlessly pursue wealth at any cost. However, as impressive as these men and women were, something about them didn't sit well with me. Many of them had a hardness about them. I couldn't put my finger on it, but their eyes were cold and their expressions edgy. They were at the top of their game, pulling in over two million dollars a year, yet many of them looked unfulfilled. Without exception they possessed a feral intensity, as if they were always on the hunt and had been since anyone could remember. For the first time in my life, it occurred to me that the choices we make have long term consequences. Not just financial ones, but emotional and mental consequences too. Perhaps by dedicating their lives to selfish ends, they were paying a price? Had they traded kindness for hard cash? Had they buried their sensitive sides for fear of showing weakness in a world that might give them everything, but could take it away in a heartbeat.

Years later, I realised we humans only have so much time and energy and what we do with both is important. If we neglect to love or be kind and only focus on selfish goals, we begin to lose touch with the best parts of ourselves. Over time our selfish ideals eat us up, but it can happen so slowly we rarely notice. Did I want to dedicate my life to the pursuit of such goals?

I should have known I was never going to fit into the financial world, but it would take a lot more suffering to show me that I was in the wrong place, doing the wrong thing, at the wrong time.

o   o   o

All the graduates passed the Series 7 exam. To celebrate, the bank rented a cruise ship to sail around Manhattan Island with us on board. Picked up from our hotel by taxi, we were driven to the port and whisked away on a luxury yacht to spend the evening drinking cocktails, dancing to cheesy seventies music and taking in the famous New York skyline.

My school report once described me as someone who, "doesn't suffer fools gladly" and "needs to learn to control his impulses better." Towing the party line, particularly when I believed the line was frayed, has never been my strong suit and that evening I made my first serious mistake in the trading world.

It was an easy mistake to avoid, but the chance to wind up a few bankers who took themselves too seriously, was too tempting to ignore. A colleague and I decided that rather than wear our pin-striped suits to the party, we would go to the ball dressed in drag; wearing figure hugging sarongs, with our faces plastered in badly done make-up. As the rest of our class drank cocktails and mingled with senior bankers in impeccable suits, we found ourselves on the edge of awkward conversations whilst dressed like two Asian ladies of the night.

The senior bankers were not impressed. Their

snide comments and cold looks made it loud and clear that humour of this kind was not appreciated at the bank. Unwilling to let a few killjoys spoil our evening, my friend and I partied in drag for the rest of the night, laughing and joking with the other graduates, whilst being willfully ignored by our bosses.

The following day I said goodbye to my room and checked out of the Lexington. New York had been my home for the last two months and the whole trip had been a grand adventure that I felt I had made the most of. As the plane to London took off, I looked down onto the land that had been kind to me and smiled. Little did I know that I was heading back to London to repay the favour my company had done for me — with blood, sweat and tears.

Chapter 4. The Bottom of the heap

"The primary cause of unhappiness is never the situation
but your thoughts about it."

– Eckhart Tolle, spiritual teacher

Working as a sales trader in London was surreal to say the least. My offices were close to St. Paul's Cathedral and the contrast between its modern glass structure and the ancient church couldn't have been greater. St. Paul's was bustling with life; an area where the old City met the new City, old money met new money and an obscene amount of both were on display. Cool bars and shops lined the streets and I couldn't count how many supercars passed by each hour. The old buildings reminded me that this part of the world had been a financial powerhouse for a very long time. The City was bigger than the people in it. A place rich in history, tradition, innovation and greed. A place where you either won big, or you went home with your tail between your legs, never to return.

I worked in our brand new, purpose-built European Head Quarters which were sleek and impressive. My office was a colossal, open plan room which stretched as far as the eye could see. There were desks for over three hundred employees. The open plan design was no mistake. It was a deliberate ploy to make sure we had nowhere to hide. It could have been confused for a semiconductor factory somewhere in the depths of Taiwan, except the workers who occupied it wore Ralph Lauren t-shirts and slacks. This office was built for efficiency and designed without so much of a hint of the feminine touch. Everything was grey or black or white and apart from the odd family photograph on some of the desks, nothing detracted from the subliminal message,

"You are here to make money, as much money as you can and don't you forget it."

When I first began, there wasn't a pot plant in sight to remind anyone that Mother Nature existed and unless you had a desk near a window, you might not see the sun all day. My desk was right in the middle of the room.

As a junior, I was one of the first people into work in the morning. There existed an unwritten, yet unnegotiable rule, that the youngest employees came to work before everyone else. They say money doesn't sleep and my co-workers paid testament to this. If I was in the office at a quarter to six in the morning, I was never alone. By seven-thirty, the room was full.

A couple of months after I had arrived back from New York I was given my own client list. I had twelve different accounts, all of them American. Small pension funds, hedge funds and a few other funds ended up on my desk. To my surprise, most of what I had learned in New York was irrelevant. I had studied economic theory, statistics and philosophy, but if I was going to make it as a sales trader, I needed more.

The best sales traders were the people who were good at dealing with people. Men and women who built relationships, could talk their way out of tricky situations and keep the right clients happy at the right time. It could be an enlivening job, with excitement, challenge and a few laughs along the way. It could also be soul destroying, depending on one's approach to the whole thing. I needed to have the right mind-set. Mental strength, nerves of steel and an unwavering commitment to slogging it out were vital to survive, otherwise the job would chew me up and spit me out, piece by piece.

Every day I called my clients early in the morning and gave them my views on what the markets were going to do that day. Sharing my ideas on how to turn their millions into billions, was not comfortable. I felt I was putting my neck on the block every day, because few things felt worse than a prediction that went wrong. If my clients liked my ideas, they would give me their business. If they didn't like them, or me, they wouldn't even take my calls. Most of them knew far more about the markets than I did. They were the experts and I was no more than a wet-nosed trainee. In a dog-eat-dog world, all the dogs were smarter than me.

In the trading game, information is money. Some of that information came from my screen, some from my phone, some from newspapers and a great deal from listening to my colleagues' conversations. I couldn't absorb everything that happened around me, but the more information I could filter out from the barrage of noise, the more useful I was.

I might be reading figures from a chart on my computer, trying to figure out which way as stock was going to move, when I would hear a colleague mention the name of another stock that one of my clients was interested in. My ears pricked up as I listened intently to the conversation, noting down anything of importance.

To catch these gems, I had to be alert, tuned in to what that was going on around me, without focusing too much on any one thing. I had to learn to be like a hawk perched on top of a telegraph pole, watching and listening for the faintest rustle of a mouse somewhere in the undergrowth. Being alert all the time wasn't easy because my brain liked to wander, but with practice I honed the ability to be present with what was going on around me. I could type an email, while talking to a client on the phone, whilst half listening to a conversation next to me. This multitasking may not sound too impressive to the ladies reading this book, but for a man to focus on more than one thing at a time was considered a great talent!

Two large TVs hung from the ceiling above my desk, blasting out all the bad news that CNN and Fox could muster. Porsche, Ferrari and Maserati car keys littered the desks around me, left in full view as a not-so-subtle reminder of what was most important here. The days varied from fast and furious to dead calm. I was at my best when the trading floor was busy.

The quiet times, which became more frequent as the markets slowed down, were funereal. I had joined the rat race towards the end of a decade long stock market boom, where everyone was used to making money. I can't remember how many months I had been working, but it was obvious that the best of it was over and we were sliding into a recession. How deep or severe, was a mystery, but the analysts had their theories and they didn't look good. We all knew that if the slump that hit in the late nineties continued, it was only a matter of time before heads rolled and bonuses vanished into thin air. I began to feel the pressure, as did most of my colleagues.

From time to time, the markets turned the wrong way, or someone made a mistake or broke a promise. These were the times when I found out if I was fit for the job or not. To my dismay, I wasn't as fit as I had hoped.

On one occasion I bought a stock instead of selling it and before I noticed my mistake the price plummeted. A minute later, the penny dropped. My stomach lurched, I leapt up and ran across the floor, barging through my co-workers to get to the trader who could rectify my mistake. I had the deal reversed, but it was too late. Within a minute and a half, I had lost a quarter of a million dollars of the bank's money.

Back at my desk, I sat with my head in my hands, feeling like the bottom had dropped out of my world. Then the voice of a senior trader came over my intercom.

"You screwed that one up, idiot," he mocked in his typically smug way. My fists tightened as my embarrassment morphed into anger. Had I been a good sales trader, I would have taken his words on the chin, apologised and got on with explaining what had happened to my boss. Instead, I sat at my desk, staring into space, fuming.

A couple of minutes later, I could hold myself back no more. I stood up and marched over to the trader, with a rage in my belly that had vanquished reason. The overweight trader was sitting at his desk, eating his second chocolate doughnut of the morning. As a child, I was the smallest of all my friends and like many small people, I had developed a bit of a temper. It had been necessary to get through life without being squashed too often. My quick temper and cutting tongue had helped me survive the jungle of an all-boys boarding school, but I had never intended to test it out on the trading floor. However the red mist had descended and I was going to take this guy on.

"What's your problem?" I spat aggressively. "I know I screwed up, but there's no need to rub my nose in it."

The senior trader turned his head towards me, doughnut crumbs clinging to his bloated chin. Looking me up and down, as if I was something he had just stood on, he placed his donut on a napkin and slowly stood up. It took him an awfully long time to get to his feet. That was when it dawned on me that I was picking a fight with one of the biggest guys on the floor. At almost six foot four, he towered over me, his arms bigger than my legs. Images of David and Goliath would have flashed before me, had I not been so angry.

"Trainees shouldn't speak to their betters like that," he drawled in a cool and unbearably arrogant voice.

Again, had I been a good sales trader, I would have backed down and offered to buy him a drink, but tact was not my *forté*, so I went for him.

"You idiot. I screwed up. I'm sorry, okay?" I growled, my tone far from apologetic.
He looked me up and down. Paused to reflect. Then decided I had a point.

"Okay," he said, nodding his head. "I won't be so hard on you again."

It wasn't an apology, but it was close enough. Luckily, the trader was the wiser man and backed down. Not because he was scared, but because he knew it was wise to have as many good relationships on the trading floor as possible. You never knew when you might need a favour or an ally to get you out of a tight spot. He even offered to buy me a drink, once more revealing why he was a senior trader and I wasn't.

I was lucky to get away with that episode. Having a short fuse was acceptable if you were making big bucks, but for a new guy it was a no-no. I was not impressed with how I had conducted myself. I had no excuse for losing my cool. After that episode, I developed a sneaking suspicion that I couldn't handle the stress of the trading floor and at some point, I would make another mistake, perhaps a bigger one?

This added pressure wasn't good for me and a feeling that something was wrong crept into the back of my mind and sat there, quietly, rarely leaving me.

Was sales trading really for me? Although I tried, I couldn't shake the feeling that I was supposed to be doing something else with my life — something more significant than becoming a money-making machine. On top of this, a fear of panic attacks returned, looming over me like a dark cloud in a stormy sky.

Chapter 5. The Traders

"The only difference between fear and excitement is your attitude towards them."

– Anon.

The sales traders on my desk were an eclectic bunch. Mike was tall and blessed with looks which could have come from Colin Firth or Nigel Havers. He was kind, honest and regarded as the best sales trader around. He was good at his job but absolutely hated it. His clients adored him, his co-workers trusted him and everyone wanted to be Mike's friend, but all Mike wanted was a quiet life in a sleepy village in the Cotswolds.

One evening Mike and I were having a few drinks in a bar when he confided in me.

"When I started out in this business, I had had a cunning plan. I was going to make more money than I ever needed, as fast as I could and get out of banking before I was too old."

Here he was, fifteen years later, still a slave to the dollar. Hearing Mike's words gave me a sinking feeling in my stomach. His plan was no different to mine and if he couldn't pull it off, how on earth could I?

Jane, a hardnosed, but kind-hearted American was the heartbeat of our sales trading team. When Jane was in a good mood, she made coming to work worthwhile and when she was on the warpath, even the bravest traders gave her a wide berth. Jane was blonde, sporty and as bright as they come. Exuding a deep confidence, she had an air of "I'll have a laugh with you, but don't mess with me. I bite."

From time to time one of the traders would take more than their fair share from one of Jane's deals and she would transform into an intensely scary being. Her sharp tongue and withering stare would tear strips off the most hardened of traders, but for some reason most of them enjoyed being told off by Jane. I think they admired her straight talking, no-nonsense approach to life. Once the admonishment was over and the deal sorted out, Jane would revert to her usual smiling self. It was poetry to watch.

My mentor was a man called Doug. Doug was a wheeler-dealer who had been in the bank for years. He hadn't been to university and had worked his way up from the bottom. A natural comedian, he loved to take the mickey out of everyone and everything. Doug was in his early forties and made no bones about being in the business for the money and nothing else. He knew of no other way to rake in so much cash and did so joyfully. Doug possessed an ability I admired greatly. He was able to laugh in the face of disaster and see the funny side of pretty much anything that went wrong. On the trading floor this quality was gold dust. Too many people took themselves too seriously, driving themselves towards an early grave worrying by too much. A trade didn't go as well as expected and their day was ruined, or a client didn't call when they said they would and they'd have a mini-meltdown. Doug was different, he sucked up chaos and unleashed his soft wit and gentle chuckle on the proceedings. This too was poetry.

My boss was cut from a different cloth. He was one of the angriest men I have ever met. A few stones overweight, with fiery red hair and a blotchy face, he stomped around the trading floor with his teeth clenched, muttering angrily to himself. His angry, red blotches flared up with his temper and his man management skills were medieval. Unlike most pessimists he didn't see the glass as half empty, he saw it as entirely unoccupied. His main pastimes were making money and flying off the handle, both of which he did on a regular basis. Complements didn't come easily and if he did have a smile on his face, it was because he was making a tonne of money, or someone he disliked was losing it. I did everything I could to avoid him.

There were many characters in that world and by far the strangest were the super-serious MBA graduates, who lived and died for their work. They rarely ate lunch, didn't smile and spoke in a dry monotone which could send you to sleep in seconds. The MBA's had a relentless, driven, intensity about them. Like the Terminator, they never rested, or took holidays, or gave up on their pursuit of financial excellence. A quick sandwich at their desk was enough to power these cyborgs for the day. I saw most of them as socially challenged beings who needed a hug, but would never have accepted one. There was no logic to hugs. Many of their interactions were performed with an air of quiet impatience, as if they were dealing with someone who had the mental capacity of an earthworm. They weren't necessarily arrogant, they just didn't get people.

Had they been allowed to, many would have slept in a secluded corner of the office, instead of wasting valuable banking time travelling to and from home. What they lacked in charisma, they made up for in Ivy League educations and as long as they were making pots of money they were tolerated.

At the other end of the spectrum were the barrow boys or East-End geezers, who had joined the bank at sixteen and worked their way up from nothing. The typical geezer was short haired, loud mouthed and sported a diamond studded earring. He wore a tight-fitting designer suit, shoes with big buckles and splashed on too much aftershave. The geezers loved being in the thick of things and spent much of the day bellowing at each other incomprehensibly, in a language that bore no resemblance to English. Their incessant barking would have got them sectioned under the Mental Health Act, had they not been so rich. Like a gang of happy football hooligans, they would chant their infamous,

"Oi, oi, oi," whenever life amused them. If someone fell over or spilt their coffee over their computer, the geezers would begin to chant. If the person then lost their cool or tried to tell them off, the chanting would escalate into a deafening roar. Except when Jane was on the war path. Then the geezers would remain respectfully quiet and silently enjoy her caustic castigations.

The geezers loved to play jokes on each other, or anyone who was foolish enough to get too close to them. Sticking "kick me" post-it's on people's backs was one of their favourites. They didn't possess what anyone would call a "sophisticated sense of humour," but their excitement and enthusiasm were infectious. They possessed a refreshing honesty. They didn't have airs and graces or worry about laughing too loudly or telling saucy jokes. Political correctness had not yet entered their domain. As long as they had someone to tease or throw paper airplanes at, they were the happiest people on the floor.

The charming geezers distrusted the socially awkward MBA's and spurned their American work ethic, taking all the boozy lunches they could get away with. The geezers relied on charm and quick wits to make their money and get what they wanted and I enjoyed their company very much.

Had I been more aware, I would have seen that once the initial excitement of my job had passed, few aspects of sales trading interested or suited me. I wasn't good with numbers, I loved being outdoors and I wasn't particularly greedy by nature. In short, I was not well suited to banking.

With three hundred people crammed into one office, the chance of someone losing their cool was high. I once saw an American equities trader throw one of his colleagues across a desk, smashing his face into a computer screen.

It all happened in a flash.

I was talking to a client on the phone when an angry yell punctured the hum of the trading floor.

"God damn it! I told you to sell," a stocky American trader shouted at a smaller colleague sitting next to him. The trading floor fell silent as three hundred people turned to watch the drama unfold. The smaller trader shot a defiant look at the angry trader, shook his head and muttered something under his breath. This further aggravated the American, who grabbed the smaller man by his jacket lapels. In one swift movement, he picked him up and threw him across his desk, pushing his face into a VDU.

Crunch.

A collective gasp went up.

With as much dignity as he could muster, the flustered victim picked himself up and straightened his tie.

"Moron," he muttered, doing a fine job of keeping his composure.

"Oi, oi, oi," the geezers began to chant in unison and the tension lifted. The two traders looked at each other and smirked.

"I'm sorry, Bill," The big American apologised, offering his hand.

"You dickhead," Bill replied.

Then they shook hands.

The traders, who were also the best of friends, were out drinking together that night, as if nothing had happened. The trading floor was that kind of a place: high tempo, high octane, high stress.

Chapter 6. Wrong place, wrong time

"For there is nothing either good or bad, but thinking makes it so."

— William Shakespear, poet.

I can't tell you the name of the bank I worked for as I had to sign a gagging order. This was presumably to stop me from bringing them into disrepute with slanderous tales of insider dealing and sexual harassment. Truth be known, I don't have any juicy stories of insider dealing and I never heard of anyone being pressured into sleeping with the boss in return for a promotion. It may have happened, though.

As my time as a sales trader stretched from weeks into months, I became steadily more discontented with work. My previous excitement for the job was replaced by a feeling of doubt that gnawed away at me. Was I in the wrong place, doing the wrong thing, at the wrong time? I wanted to embrace my job, but I couldn't shake off the feeling I was supposed to do something else with my life — something significant, but what that was? I had no idea.

Every weekday morning, I crawled out of bed at some ungodly hour, grabbed a bite to eat, pulled on my work clothes and hopped on my bright, red Piaggio Sfera scooter to ride to the bank. Before six o'clock in the morning, the roads of London were quiet, so I was able to guide my chariot through them unhindered. Riding a scooter on those empty streets was the highlight of my day.

Pulling out of my driveway, my mind disengaged from its usual grumbles and a smile appeared on my face. With the sights and sounds of London rushing by, I raced down the straights and carved my way through the curves that led to the old City; my head empty of everyday worries as a sense of freedom replaced the incessant thinking I normally experienced. This freedom was alert and aware and beyond thinking. Even if I had wanted to, I couldn't really think because if I thought too much when I was on that scooter, I would surely crash. So, I drove from instinct rather than my mind.

I didn't know it at the time, but I was experiencing a state of pure awareness and it felt fantastic. I was later to discover this state is the doorway to true happiness, but at the time I had no idea what was going on. All I knew was I enjoyed those scooter rides tremendously.

I bombed over Battersea Bridge, along the banks of the Thames, past the Houses of Parliament and Big Ben, before arriving in the old City. Five days a week, I scooted past some of the most spectacular landmarks in the world and loved every moment of it.

However, as my time at the bank went on, the stresses of work caught up with me and I became more consumed by my thoughts. The state of alertness faded and the sense of freedom dulled. It sounds strange, but after a few months as a sales trader, I was no longer on the back of my scooter when I carved through the traffic. I was somewhere else in my mind. Yes, I was physically sitting on the bike, but in my head, I was at work figuring out how I was going to schmooze my clients or arguing with my boss.

I am embarrassed to write that I often lost those imaginary arguments and replayed them over and over in my mind, until I won. Sometimes it took a few attempts, but ultimately, I always came up with a witty retort or intelligent argument that dazzled my clients or impressed my boss...

I think I needed to get out more!

The thoughts in my head stole my attention, yet were of little use to me They contradicted themselves, they changed their mind, they exaggerated and lied. I felt compelled to think about my future, but no good ever came of it.

46

Those rides had invigorated my soul, but now I rarely noticed the beauty around me or the curves which had enthralled me. I was so distracted I have no idea how I made it to work in one piece and on more than one occasion I nearly didn't.

When I got to the City I should have been present with whatever was in front of me, but instead I started daydreaming about what I was going to do after work.

"Where shall I go out?"
"What's the name of that great restaurant?"
"Will the cute girl from HR be there?"
"Will she like me?"

There came a stage where my mind was so busy, I was rarely present with anything I did. My body was there, sitting in the fancy restaurant with clients, but I was somewhere else in my head, thinking about other things. As my teeth chewed on the finest lobster in London, my mind would chew over thoughts in my head. I'm not sure I appreciated a single bite.

If I had been in a different headspace, the trading floor could have been an invigorating place to be. News broke from the other side of the world and the stock market juddered. Shares shot up or plunged down and we had to take split second decisions without knowing all the facts. The market was alive, a living entity, but I couldn't enjoy it when I wasn't there. Of course, my body was sitting at my desk, but as had been the case when I was on the back of my scooter, my mind was somewhere else. My thoughts stealing my attention away from what was occurring right in front of me.

When I left work each day — you guessed it — I wasn't present either. I was busy reviewing what had happened that day or planning the next day's work. I was addicted to thinking. So addicted I couldn't stop, even when I wanted to. I spent too much time swimming around in the thoughts in my head, but back then I had no idea it could be any other way. My addiction to thinking was the root of many of my problems, dare I say *all* of them. But what could I do? I had no idea how to stop.

The pressure, which had at first exhilarated me, now sat as a knot in my stomach. The long days sitting in front of computers took their toll. I wanted to quit, but I didn't.

Every week the pressure mounted, twisting the knot tighter and giving me a gaunt and ashen look. Getting out of bed in the morning was harder and looking at myself in the bathroom mirror more harrowing. The thoughts in my head kept battering away,

"God, you look terrible."
"Look, wrinkles — you're getting old."
"No-one fancies you."

So, why did I stick at it? Why not resign? Put it all down to experience and move on?

Well, I was unwilling to miss out on what I thought was my chance to be rich and therefore happy. I was convinced that a house on a beach in Thailand was my best shot at finding what I wanted. Yet fate's noose was tightening around my neck, pushing me to learn that being at peace was not about the perfect future. I wish someone had told me that true happiness was about right now, but I don't think anyone around me knew. What was clear, was that by living for tomorrow I was becoming more and more unhappy today.

o   o   o

Initially, my plan had seemed quite brilliant. Become a trader in the City, work hard for a decade, rake in an obscene amount of cash, buy a place on the beach in Thailand and live happily ever after. This plan was what got me up at five o'clock in the morning, when all I wanted to do was roll over and go back to sleep. This plan was what bound me to a career that didn't agree with me. But surely a life on the white beaches of Ko Samui was worth the sacrifice? A decade wasn't that long, was it?

With hindsight, my plan had a great deal in common with one of Baldrick in Blackadder's cunning plans. Like the innocent Baldrick, I displayed an unwavering belief in my own plan and, no matter how ridiculous life got, the thought it might end in failure never crossed my mind.

For my cunning plan to work, I needed to

make a lot of money and if I didn't make it as a sales trader, how could I? I didn't have the confidence to start my own business and if I moved to another well-paid job in the City, what would be different? No, the beach house in Thailand was my only hope. I had to keep going. But who was I kidding? By living for tomorrow, I was getting more and more miserable today.

I considered myself a fortunate person. Throughout my life, I had a roof over my head, a loving family, plenty of friends and enough money, but had I been happy? At times, yes, but my happiness was dependent on how my life was going. If life wasn't going well, I felt unhappy. If a girl rejected me, or I got ill, or I didn't get my own way, I felt frustrated or disheartened.

In those days success was everything to me. If I wasn't successful who would respect me? Who would love me? Who would want to be with me?

As soon as I achieved one goal, I would set another. I enjoyed having goals, but mistakenly believed their fulfillment would fulfill me. With each success came a period of relief which lasted no more than a week or two. Then I was back on the hunt for another goal to chase. None of them gave me any of the permanent satisfaction I craved. I felt like a rat on a wheel, unable to hop off. If I stopped running, who knows what would become of me?

Those who knew me in passing thought I was happy because I had a cheerful, outgoing personality, but I had no inner stability and no sense of inner security. I had experienced bouts of deep depression and destructive manias and I had bounced back. However, in terms of pure, uncaused happiness, I was an amateur. So, when it came to making life decisions based on what would bring me more joy and peace, I was lost at sea. I had a feeling life offered so much more than I was experiencing, but I didn't know what that could be or how to find it.

One night, I lay in bed, staring at the blackness behind my eyelids, waiting to fall asleep. I so wanted to sleep, but my head wouldn't let me. Thoughts and ideas bounced around my mind like balls bearings in a pinball machine, leaving no space to relax and drop into the relief of unconscious slumber. All I could think about was work; my colleagues, my boss, my clients, the intern who smiled at me. Planning, analysing, regretting. I fantasised about the future and visited my pad on the beach in Thailand; my mind never stopped. My biggest dream had become my greatest burden.

Chapter 7. Humbled by life

"I'll never put off till tomorrow what I can possibly do – the day after."

– Oscar Wilde, poet.

Some people's life-changing stories are brave and heroic. Against the odds, they muster up great reserves of internal courage, take a risk and it all pays off in the end. I, on the other hand, wasn't remotely heroic. I had wanted to leave my job for a year and a half, but still hadn't thrown in the towel. Instead of quitting, I moaned a lot.

I moaned to my friends, my family and anyone else who would hear my tales of woe. If they would have listened to me, I would have moaned to strangers on the Tube. It was an undignified time.

"I hate my job, but I can't quit. There's no way I'll get a better one," I repeated, too many times to remember.

"Just quit," my friends told me. "Being happy is more important than a job."

But I wouldn't. I wanted someone else to make the decision for me because I didn't have the nerve to do it myself. Moaning fed my ego and made me feel a little better, but was at best a sticky plaster stuck over a festering sore. At some point, the sore would need to be lanced.

One evening after work, I chanced upon a photograph picturing me on my first day at work in Canary Wharf. I was dressed in a smart, dark blue, pin-striped suit with a big grin across my face. Squinting at the photo, I hardly recognised the guy looking back at me. I took the photo to the bathroom mirror and held it up next to my reflection. I was stunned. My once healthy face was now drawn and pale. I had lost weight and the sparkle in my eyes was all but gone. How could my appearance have changed so much in such a short time?

"Enough is enough. I needed to take some time off."

My decision wasn't the most courageous of affairs. I didn't storm into my boss's office, give him a piece of my mind and throw in the towel. Instead, I thought it best to hang onto my job for another four months so I could collect my Christmas bonus. The day after this bonus landed in my bank account, I would quit. I promised myself, I would quit. Until then, I would make an appointment with my doctor to get some time off work.

o o o

Walking into the doctor's surgery with a pre-prepared sob story in my mind, I sat down, preparing for the worst.

"Hmm. Well, I need to make sure you actually need sick leave," the doctor told me without looking up from her papers. "Orders from above, I'm afraid."

I took a deep breath, ready to unleash an Oscar winning performance, which would melt the hardest doctor's heart.

"So, what job do you do?"

"I'm a trader in the City."

"Two or three weeks?" she asked, without batting an eyelid.

I flew back to my parents' home in Scotland to take stock of my situation. I felt relieved. Some time away from the financial world and a few honest discussions with my parents was what I needed to see the wood from the trees and for me to get my life back on track.

I slept for a couple of days and then we talked about work, life, my future and what they thought about it all. It pained me to let go of the prestige of working in the City, but deep down I knew I had to. As a budding Dick Whittington, I had failed and as much as I hated to admit it, the time to call it a day had arrived. Mixing that highly stressful environment and a serious bipolar diagnosis, was playing with fire. It seemed that delaying my departure by four months to get the Christmas bonus, was too long to wait. I so wanted that money, but was it worth my mental health?

The moment I made my decision to quit, a lead weight was lifted from my shoulders. The tension in my face relaxed and the tight knot in my stomach loosened. For the first time in three years, I felt human again. If I could have done a backflip, I would have.

o   o   o

When I took the train from Wimbledon into work to hand in my notice, the rain was pouring down. Looking out of the window at the looming, coal-stained structure of Battersea Power Station, I felt nervous. My hands were clammy and my mouth dry. I hoped I was doing the right thing.

"Am I ready to throw away the opportunity of a lifetime?"

"Maybe I should hang on until Christmas? I can do that."

"Nope, I'm quitting."

My mobile phone woke me from my thoughts. It was my father and he sounded happy.

"Ollie, it's Daddy here," he announced, his voice booming. "Have you seen the FT this morning?"

"No," I replied. The Financial Times was the last paper I was going to read that day.

"Well, your bank is offering voluntary redundancy to all their staff. If you hold off for a week or two, they'll pay you to leave."

"Really?" I asked, not allowing myself to get too excited, "Are you sure?"

"Yes. Today's not a good day to resign," he chuckled.

As the train pulled into Clapham High Street, I leapt onto the platform, jogged to a newsstand and bought the last copy of the Financial Times I have ever purchased.

My father was right. Within a couple of weeks every single employee of my bank would be offered a payout. Today most certainly wasn't the day to resign. I was aghast. I seemed like my decision to leave was being rewarded by the angels. I could quit within the next two weeks and still get a bonus. That evening I went out for a slap-up meal at Bentley's fish restaurant in Mayfair with a great friend. Food had never tasted so good.

A few days later, I walked into my boss' office and signed an agreement promising never to darken the bank's doors ever again. That should have been the end of my rocky relationship with corporate America, but the very next day he called me.

"I'd like you to come into the office to have a chat," he said.

My heart sank.

o   o   o

"I'm sorry it didn't work out Ollie," my boss told me in a rare moment of compassion, "but I understand why you resigned. You're not the same guy who started working here. You were full of life when you arrived, but these days you seem strained and you've lost weight."

Hearing what I already knew, from a man who had worked in the business for twenty years was reassuring. "You know, some people aren't cut out for this job, they have other things to do with their life."

"Thanks," I nodded. "You're right. I'm not cut out for this, but I don't know what I am cut out for. I need a rest and hopefully I'll figure it out."

"Anyway, Ollie," he continued, beginning to feel uneasy with the openness of our conversation, "back to business. I would like you to come in for the next few weeks to make sure nothing falls through the cracks? We need to hand over your clients and make your transition as smooth as possible. It's the least you owe me."

That was the boss I knew. I could have left him in the lurch, but I agreed to help. It seemed like the decent thing to do.

Now the pressure was off, work was more enjoyable than it had ever been. I was able to relax and take long lunch breaks. Every day I walked into the City, taking time to enjoy the magnificent architecture and the feel of the place. I remember sitting in the gardens of a beautiful little chapel in the middle of the City, enjoying a double latte and a warm, melted cheese sandwich, wondering why I hadn't done this more often. I rang each of my clients to tell them I was leaving and a surprising number of them were sad to see me go. I had apparently done a better job than I had given myself credit for.

Then, out of the blue, I got an unexpected call from my favourite client which sent me into a tailspin.

"Hey Oliver, a few of the guys at work have been talking and we have a question for you," he announced in his broad Boston accent.

"Sure, Brad, ask away."

"We want to hire you. We're hoping you can help us set up an office in London. We want you to come work for us."

"Wow!"

"That's, erm, I didn't, erm, expect that," I stammered.

"We'll pay you more than they're paying you now, a lot more. We want to train you up in New York, on our night trading desk and when you're ready you can be our front man in the U.K. You can help us set up our trading base in London."

The offer was incredible. I was getting the chance to build and head up an office in Covent Garden, one of the hippest parts of London. In a weird *déjà vu*, I was once more being offered a job in finance, training in Manhattan and the chance to make even more money. How could I turn it down?

"Can you give me a couple of days to think about it?" I asked.

"No problem, Ollie. Let us know by Friday."

o   o   o

Friday came and I accepted the job, on the condition I could take three months off before I started. I wanted to recharge my batteries before I re-enter the lion's den.

Brad agreed.

Now, I *really* had it all. A redundancy cheque of nearly twenty thousand pounds, three months to do whatever I wanted and a guaranteed top job at the end of it. With regards to the capitalist values of the financial services industry, I was a seriously lucky guy.

I enjoyed my time off, but the closer I got to the end of my three-month sabbatical, the more uneasy I became. My new job weighed heavily on my mind.

"Was I doing the right thing?
"Was I up to the job?"

A wise man once said the definition of insanity is doing the same thing over and over and expecting a different result. With hindsight, I would tend to agree.

Chapter 8. Jump!

"If I hadn't seen such riches, I could live with being poor."

James, nineties pop-band.

September 2002, Cape Town, South Africa. Table Mountain stood in front of me, a symbol of beauty and strength, two qualities enjoyed by many of its peoples. I was sipping a beer in a gardened terrace with Jason, one of my closest friends when he said something that, at the time, I wish he hadn't.

"So, what about this skydiving you've been talking about. You want to do it?"

I didn't. I had no desire to throw myself out of a perfectly good plane.

"*No way,*" I thought.

"Okay," I said.

Jason gulped and nodded back at me, doing his best to look relaxed.

Neither of us wanted to skydive as we both had an aversion to heights, particularly heights over three metres. "It's not the jump that'll kill you, it's hitting the ground," I joked nervously, hoping Jason would call the whole thing off and I could finish my beer without losing face.

There was no way Jason was backing down.

"We have two choices," he issued. "If we're quick, we can get to the jump site before they close today, or," he paused, "we could do it tomorrow?"

I looked at him and then at my still half-full beer.

"Let's do it now," I declared, unwilling to spend a sleepless night tossing and turning and worrying about the jump.

Less than an hour later, we arrived at an aircraft hangar a few miles outside Cape Town. The "airport" was built in the dusty, patchwork quilt of Savannah which surrounds much of the city. Getting out of our hire car we were greeted by a burly South African with a limp.

"He's got a limp," I whispered.

"I know. Shut up," Jason hissed back.

"Driving here is far more dangerous than jumping out of the plane," the guy with limp reassured us, but I couldn't take my eyes off his leg.

"Do you think he hurt it driving to work?" I muttered.

"Shut up!"

The guy with a limp gave us a brief introduction to parachuting and before we knew it, we were strapped into our harnesses. I didn't need any more fuel on the fire of fear that was consuming me, but the arrival of our transport to the heavens added plenty.

The tiny, battered, rusted wreck of an airplane which chugged its way out of the hangar and spluttered to a halt in front of us looked incapable of taking off, let alone landing.

"Oh shit!" we thought instantaneously.

The plane had been built in the 1950's and looked like it hadn't been serviced since. To make matters worse the pilot was a little too overexcited for my liking. His eyes bulging too far out of his head and his movements manic and twitchy.

"One too many jumps," Jason whispered.

I shook my head.

Ten minutes later, we were crammed into the back of the plane, sitting cross legged on the hard metal floor.

"We've taken out the seats, so the plane is lighter," an instructor shouted over the noise of the engine.

"Whatever," I thought. *"More like someone's torn them out in a fit of hysteria."*

With myself, Jason and two instructors crammed into the back, the plane chugged down the runway, limping off the tarmac at its second attempt.

"Don't worry," an instructor shouted, "we've done this hundreds of times."

I really wanted to be somewhere else. Anywhere else would have been just fine.

"What happens if one of us doesn't jump?" I asked. "Do you fly us back down?"

"They always jump," the instructor smiled. "Sometimes they just need a bit of encouragement." The way he said the word "encouragement" left me in no doubt this was a firm kick in the backside. "Besides, this plane won't land with more than the pilot in it. It's too old," he shouted as an afterthought.

"Great."

The little plane rode the Savannah's thermals upwards, climbing higher and higher. As it did, I began to feel different. Circling up and up, slowly bumping our way towards the heavens, the nervous chatter in my head subsided and I began to feel peaceful. I didn't know why, but perhaps the enormity of what I was about to do was calming my overactive mind. Even the prospect of being "encouraged" to leave the plane wasn't scary anymore.

"I could get used to this," I thought, and then…

Bang.

My new-found inner calm shattered as one of the instructor's boots kicked the plane door open. A deafening wind rushed in, shaking my nerves with it's terrible roar. Before I knew it, Jason and his instructor had edged their way to the open door.

Then they were gone.

Now there were two of us, but somehow, I felt very alone. But what could I do? I was sitting in a plane which couldn't land, strapped to an instructor who wouldn't take "no" for an answer. We shuffled towards the open door and swung our feet out of the plane. I sat with my legs dangling in midair and my eyes scanning the ground below. I should have been terrified, but as the patchwork quilt stared up at me, I felt no fear at all.

"Three... two... one... go!"
Myself and my instructor rolled headfirst out of the plane...

The next three seconds were the most spectacular of my life.
I was weightless, formless, free of thought and everyday concerns.
There was no fear, no problems.
I was space, I was presence and it was divine.
The experience of being alive was incredible.
My mind still, clear and aware.

For a few seconds I had an experience of pure awareness. A silent sense of absolute aliveness. I was experiencing life as it was happening right now and it had never felt so good.

As our parachute opened and the intensity of the experience diminished, the sense of freedom faded, but a hint of it remained for days.

I landed safely, knowing I had gone through something which had changed my life. After that parachute jump, I was different. I had tasted a new state of consciousness. I now knew what it was like to be free. The jump had disconnected me from my horrible mind and connected me to a state of presence. Now I had tasted this presence and there was no turning back. The lyrics of a James song came to mind.

"If I hadn't seen such riches, I could live with being poor."

I had been given a gift that had opened my eyes wider. A switch had been flicked and I wasn't going to rest until I experienced that presence again. If I could experience it once surely it could happen again and again?

I hoped so.

o   o   o

Three months passed all too quickly and once again I found myself on a plane, this time a British Airways 747 flying to New York. I am a great believer that life has a way of showing us the things we need to see; and if we don't see them, life slaps us in the face with them until we do.

The first sign that I was moving in the wrong direction came when I checked into my accommodation in New York. Unlike the four-star Lexington, this was far from luxurious. Standing outside a high-rise motel with my suitcase in one hand and a copy of the Wall Street Journal in another, I felt uneasy. The scruffy motel looked like it had come straight out of an American gangster movie. Walking inside, my doubts were confirmed. Behind the reception slouched a grouchy porter, who didn't look up until I had rung the buzzer in front of him three times. The poor man seemed numbed by a boredom that only years of monotony can bring. When he finally spoke to me, he pulled each of his words out of a deep, dark hole inside himself as if each one weighed more than he could bear.

"No smoking in the rooms, no noise after ten thirty, no call girls, no fighting," he sighed. "Here's your keys. If you lose them, it'll cost you twenty bucks. If you cause any problems, you'll be thrown off the premises and you won't get your money back." He paused, holding my gaze but remaining stony-faced. "You understand?"

"Erm, yes?"

"Then sign here," he demanded.

I signed and without another word the porter returned to his seat and his state of perpetual boredom. This was not a promising start.

My wristwatch showed one o'clock in the afternoon. Taking the lift to the eleventh floor, I was met by a group of characters skulking around the corridor, drinking scotch and smoking roll-ups. Clear evidence that none of the other guests had taken the porter's words too seriously. To get to my room, I had to squeeze past drug dealers, wannabe gangster rappers and ladies of the night. It was quite something!

That night, I was woken by the bloodcurdling screams of a couple on the floor above me. It sounded like a body part was being slammed against the floor over and over again. The noise eventually stopped and was replaced by an eerie silence. I strained my ears, but heard nothing. Either the couple had just had extraordinarily passionate sex, or someone had been murdered — I never found out which. I fell asleep with a sense of fearful foreboding.

o   o   o

The following evening, I met one of my co-workers, Chuck, in a bar. Chuck was handsome, well-dressed and on his way to becoming a very wealthy man. He spent his nights trading and his weekends bedding any pretty woman who was naïve enough to fall for his charm. Just by opening his mouth, Chuck revealed he was more than just a little full of himself. His only topics of conversation were boasting about the last woman he bedded or banging on about one of his recent "killer" trades. He talked of nothing else. On that first evening, my new best-buddy in New York, spent two long hours telling me how amazing he was. I cringed.

That evening I walked into my new offices and spent the night learning their trading system. Sitting in front of those computer screens, as Chuck taught me the new trading system, was mind numbing. I was jet-lagged and didn't understand anything he told me. Then it dawned on me, I had made a terrible mistake. The hard truth was staring me in the face, but this time I couldn't avoid it. For the second time in my career, I was in the wrong place, doing the wrong thing at the wrong time.

At six o'clock in the morning, I took my suit jacket from the back of my chair, nodded to Chuck and left the building.

"See you at O'Leary's, we've got some chicks to pull," he shouted after me.

I didn't reply.

Even though my wallet was begging me to stay, I couldn't do it. Even though the beach house in Thailand was only a few years of hard work away, I couldn't do it. No part of me could begin the journey of pretending all over again. Struggling on at the bank, knowing it wasn't for me, had been one thing, but embarking on another, equally undesirable financial career would have beyond the pale.

The next day I flew back to the UK and quit.

Chapter 9. Help comes in mysterious ways

"Wherever I go, whatever I do, I take me with me."
– Hazell Dean, pop singer.

Though the title of this book might imply that I found happiness by quitting my job, casting off my responsibilities and skipping off into the sunset; nothing could be further from the truth.

After a few weeks enjoying a tremendous sense of relief, I found myself back where I had begun — restless, bored and living a life with little meaning or purpose. I had time, money and friends and lived in a beautiful flat in one of the poshest areas of London, but I wasn't satisfied. I was less stressed than I had been in the bank, but was I any happier?

No.

Slowly, the idea that something was wrong,

began to claw its way back into my psyche. I wasn't at peace and felt no closer to my goal. Perhaps I was even further away from happiness because I was no longer receiving the healthy pay cheques every month.

Feeling disheartened, I went for a stroll on Wimbledon Common with my Sony Discman plugged into my ears. On an occasion such as this, only one band was going to do the trick:

Westlife.

For some reason, few of my friends recognised the genius that lay behind this boy band. The slow-motion shots of band members expressing the pain of lost love, or the black and white images of glistening teeth, singing soul-searching lyrics were lost on them, but touched me to my core. I guess as far as music was concerned, I was a cheap date.

The Irish boy band were just what I needed to get myself into a suitably melancholic mood, as my feet padded along the soft grass and my mind wandered between lost loves and lost opportunities.

I had taken medication for bipolar for a few years. Thankfully, it had kept the worst of the illness at bay, but it dampened my ability to feel. Only when my emotions were strong did I feel them and today was such a day. Tears flowed down my cheeks as some of the pent-up emotion which had sat inside me for the last few years erupted. I hoped I wouldn't bump into anyone I knew.

"Why is this happening to me?"
"Why am I not happy?"
"I've tried to be a good person."

Since I was small, I had believed in God. This was somewhat surprising, considering that as a child, I had been subjected to the fire-and-brimstone sermons of an overenthusiastic Episcopalian minister. Images of that red-faced man preaching damnation and hellfire from the safety of his pulpit came to me. In case anyone in the congregation didn't already possess a strong enough sense of religious guilt, he was there to make sure we all knew that God disapproved of pretty much everything we had ever done.

Hammock's sermons should have bound me in fear of eternal damnation. Yet, despite being threatened with endless suffering for such serious crimes as swearing or missing Sunday school, I never believed a word he said. It is fascinating how children can sniff out an idiot well before many adults can. My version of God was the opposite to his. To me, God was kind, someone who watched over me like a protective parent, full of love.

So, as I strolled around Wimbledon common, walking in time to the beat of one of Westlife's more touching tracks and wiping the tears from my eyes, I prayed.

"Please help me. I'm lost. This isn't working. Show

me what I am meant to do with my life. Please show me what to do."

I usually said a prayer when the shit hit the fan. However, this prayer was different. Only a couple of years earlier I had thought I knew it all, I was invincible. That arrogance had been beaten out of me by the kind of tough love that only life dishes out. Not only was my prayer accompanied by *Queen of my Heart*, but for the first time in many years, I was genuinely humble. I needed help because I was lost — utterly lost — and I knew it. On that overcast afternoon, alone on Wimbledon Common, the cocky young guy disappeared and his cry for help came from the very bottom of his heart.

o   o   o

Four days later, I found myself in the hands of a shiatsu practitioner in Edinburgh. As he pressed his thumbs into my tension filled body, I squealed like a stuck pig. Throughout the treatment he talked about a type of meditation he did. All I wanted was a massage, not a lecture on inner peace. But I kept quiet as he continued to share his enthusiasm, using words like "enlightenment" and "chakras." I had no idea what he was talking about.

Once the massage was over, I thanked him and shook his hand, assuring him I would look into this meditation business. Then I left, with no intention of doing any such thing.

Despite my cynicism, this kind man was offering me a gift. My prayer from only days before was being answered, but I didn't see it that way.

"If you learn Ascension," he had told me in a broad Scottish accent. "It will give you more peace and joy and it will make your life easier." His words piqued my curiosity and somewhere deep inside, I knew this Ascension could be for me. But I had better things to do with my life than sit cross-legged for hours on end, trying to silence my mind. I filed meditation away with a long list of things I should do, but never would.

Life continued much as before, with me feeling disillusioned with myself, society and the world. I continued to bang my head against a wall; whinging and moaning about wanting to be happy, but doing nothing about it. Luckily, this world is a friendlier place than I appreciated back then. Even though I was too stubborn to do anything about finding peace, life was going to hammer me, and hammer me and hammer me until I did.

Chapter 10. Mountain rescue

"Chasing angels or fleeing demons, go to the mountains."

– Jeffrey Rasley, author.

Two weeks later, I found myself driving along the M4 motorway towards Wales; the land of daffodils and dragons, with an old university friend called Matt. We had decided to spend a few days in the mountains of Snowdonia and were excited about the adventure that lay ahead. What better way to blow London's cobwebs away?

At university, Matt had been the life and soul of the party. A huge man, he had an uncanny ability to sniff out both chaos and adventure wherever he went; and if life got too serious, he was the one cracking jokes and taking the edge off things.

It was a warm midsummer's morning, when we drove from our hostel to the foot of one of the highest mountains in Wales, Carnedd Llewelyn, intent on climbing to the top of it. The weather was hot, so we wore shorts and T-shirts. There wasn't a cloud in the sky, so our Gortex jackets stayed in the car. We might get hungry, so we packed a bag of crisps and a Mars bar. We needed to know where we were going, so a button compass (the sort one finds in a Christmas cracker) and an un-laminated map came with us too. It was the middle of June and the thermometer was pushing twenty-five, what could possibly go wrong?

I considered myself a competent navigator. Having spent three whole weeks learning how to read a map at the Royal Military Academy in Sandhurst, I was in no doubt we could find our way into the mountains and back home again in time for tea. Unfortunately, my navigational incompetence was matched only by the depth of my self-delusion. I conveniently forgot I had nearly failed the Officers' training course, due to my poor map reading skills. I had only managed to scrape through my orienteering exam, by following an Officer Cadet from the Parachute Regiment who knew what he was doing. If it hadn't been for his expertise, I would still be running around the Wiltshire countryside with a confused look on my face. Quite honestly, I could have got lost in a paper bag if I wasn't careful.

Three hours into our hike, things were going well. Having clambered almost two thirds of the way up the side of the mountain, we found ourselves on a more level patch of ground as we walked the length of a wide ridge. I turned to Matt and smirked at the sight of this enormous man hiking his way into the wilds of Snowdonia in bright, yellow Bermuda shorts.

That was when I saw it. Lurking in the distance. A sinister and foreboding sight which took the wind right out of my sails.

"Oh shit."

Far into the distance, a line of angry storm clouds was rolling towards us at a furious rate. They were many miles away, but I could see the dark greys and blues, tumbling and swirling ferociously across the sky, like a scene from the *Lord of the Rings*. So much for mid-June: I had never seen such an ominous sky, which was turning blacker by the minute; twisted and distorted by a force which had our number on it.

Matt saw the look of horror on my face and turned around.

"We have got to get off this mountain," he said. Hastily, we discussed our options and decided we had only three:

1. We could stay where we were and die.
2. We could retrace our steps, clamber down the steep mountainside we had hiked up and probably die.
3. We could try to find a route down the slope to our left and possibly die.

If we had had the right equipment, the first

option could have been fun, minus the dying part. We could have found some shelter, pitched a tent in the lee of a pile of stones, cooked ourselves a hearty meal and waited out the storm. But we didn't have a tent and we had already drunk our water and eaten our crisps.

Retracing our steps would take us back to the car, but it meant heading straight into the storm. If the storm hit us whilst we were making our descent, the terrain would become impossibly slippery. Climbing down is far harder than climbing up and one false move would be the end of us.

The third choice was a mystery, but with my expert map-reading skills, we might make it down before the worst of the storm hit. What we didn't appreciate was that the slope to our left was littered with cliffs and if we didn't get our navigation bang on, we would need a rope and harness to get down. We had neither.

Then the wind blew up and it began to rain. A few splatters soon became a tropical downpour and our options shrank further. Matt and I looked at each other, neither of us wanting to make the final decision. When you are caught between the devil and the deep blue sea, which do you choose?

"Let's toss a coin," I suggested.

"No, let's be grown-ups," Matt replied sternly. Two minutes later we were heading towards the mountainside to our left, hoping for the best.

On those mountains the temperature can drop unnaturally fast and it did. If we had packed more food and some warm, waterproof clothes, we would have been fine. If we had possessed a decent compass, we might have been okay too, but our Christmas cracker compass wouldn't even take a bearing. A horrible feeling of foreboding invaded the pit of my stomach. The feeling that comes with losing control. We were at the mercy of the elements and the elements were not having a merciful day. I hoped I wouldn't have a panic attack.

Each time we found a route which might lead us to safety, we hit cliffs we couldn't get past. We would then turn around and hike back up the mountain, hoping for a better route to appear fifty metres along the ridge. We did this again and again and again, each time hitting a wall of stone which dropped into oblivion below us.

At some point, the wind died down and a dense carpet of whitish-grey fog came in, so thick we couldn't tell how high the cliffs were because we couldn't see the ground below us. All sight of the valley was lost in this impenetrable mist and although we were no longer in danger of being blown off the mountain, the chance of walking off the edge of a cliff was now a real danger.

Our map was soaked, impossible to read and our clothes now drenched. Our stylish beachwear offered no warmth and our easygoing smiles were a distant memory. Bright yellow Bermuda shorts may have a certain appeal in Surfers' Paradise, but not up a mountain in Wales. They now clung to our legs like damp sponges, sucking the heat from our skin.

"If you die first, I'm going to eat you," Matt quipped and I smiled. For a while he cracked jokes to keep our spirits up, but as our bodies began to freeze, our conversation died down to an intimidating silence.

From time to time, both of us exchanged concerned looks, but neither wanted to admit to how scared we were. Matt, who was wearing the fewest clothes, was starting to get very cold indeed. His head went down and his pace slowed, as the initial stages of exposure began to set in. I wasn't far behind. Both of us knew enough about the mountains, to know we didn't know enough about these mountains to turn this thing around. We were way out of our depth and paying the price for our stupidity.

I remember passing an old wooden bothy. This ramshackle old hut had a half-collapsed roof, but it offered some shelter.

"We can stay in there until the weather improves," I suggested.

"No way," Matt growled, "If I stop now, I won't start again. If we don't get off this bloody mountain, we'll freeze to death — bothy, or no bothy."

With those words, coming from a man who found it easy to make light of the gravest disasters, the seriousness of our situation hit me hard. We were already heading towards exposure and if we stopped to rest, one or both of us might fall asleep and never wake up. It was not the worst way to go, but we didn't have any plans on going just yet.

Then the hail came in. Pellets of ice battered us from the heavens. I hoped the fog would lift, as it usually does when the wind comes in.

It didn't.

o   o   o

As time passed, our plight was getting steadily worse. The colder we became, the more intense our rising panic. The more intense our panic the more fatigued we became. It was physically exhausting to walk up and down the mountain in sodden clothes, but the mental exhaustion of pushing away the fear of death was worse. The storm wasn't passing. If anything, the weather was intensifying. I prided myself in being able to figure my way out of most of the messes I got myself into, but today I had no answer. Nothing could be done, other than keep going and try to ignore the stark fact that we were marching towards our doom. I was so afraid. I just wanted to jump on the ground, hammer the wet stones with my fists and burst into tears. Perhaps a route down would appear? But perhaps it wouldn't?

I looked to Matt for reassurance, but I could see he was thinking the same as me. We tried to encourage each other, but both of us were screaming on the inside, doing a poor job of quelling our rising panic. On the mountain that day, I felt so small, like a pawn in a game I couldn't control. I only had one option left.

I prayed. I prayed as hard as I could.

"Please God, get me out of this. I don't want to die. I'll do good with my life. I'll help people. Just get us off this mountain alive."

Peering into the fog, I frantically hoped some form of salvation would arrive, but it didn't. So, we trudged on, stumbling, sometimes falling to our knees. I wondered how long we could keep going and which of us would be the first to fall to the ground and not get up. I didn't fancy my chances of carrying Matt anywhere and neither of us would leave the other on the mountain alone.

Then something happened. Something I will never forget. Something magical. Something miraculous. If you are one of those cynical types who doesn't believe in magic, you might call this coincidence. I call it a miracle.

Just as I was picking myself up from another stumble on the rocks, I looked ahead, expecting to see the same sea of fog I had stared into for the last hour, but a flash of blue caught my attention. Then it disappeared. There, again, a flash of blue not far from us. Then it vanished into the mist, so quickly I wasn't sure if I had imagined it. I kept on staring.

Nothing.

"Did you see that?" I shouted to Matt.

"See what?"

Before I could reply, a gap appeared in the fog and a blue silhouette, which could have been a person revealed itself. Then a red silhouette and then five more.

o   o   o

Ahead of us, out of the fog, appeared a group of climbers: seven men and women dressed in waterproofs, with rucksacks on their backs. They had all the professional kit we should have been carrying. They were proper climbers, not jokers like us. In fact, they were no ordinary climbers — they were a mountain rescue team on a training exercise!

We hadn't seen another soul all day and in our darkest hour we met a group of trained mountain experts. I looked to the heavens — well, at least as far as the fog would allow me — and uttered an almost silent,

"Thank you."

Matt's expression was that of a man who had been nibbled and then spared by the jaws of death. My own relief contrasted sharply with the mountain rescue team's disapproving looks. They had seen it all before; young guys without proper equipment, showing no common sense or respect for nature. Cocksure idiots who underestimated the elements and paid the price for their ignorance.

"You were lucky you bumped into us," one of them told me through gritted teeth.

He was right. Matt and I apologised all the

way down the mountain. A descent the mountain rescue team made look simple.

In thirty minutes, we were down in the valley floor. After a quick check over, they found Matt was suffering from mild hypothermia and I was very cold. As we made our way back to the car, heads hanging and teeth chattering, our pride hurt more than anything.

Within three hours, I had warmed up in a hot bath and eaten some scampi and chips. We had been foolhardy, but at least the shock had put things into perspective for me. Lying in that gloriously hot bath, I thought deeply about our near miss on the mountain. If I had died up there, would I have been happy with the life I had led? Would I have been able to look the angels, or the saints, or whoever was going to meet me at the Pearly Gates, in the eye and say,

"Yes, I did what I was meant to do. I was a good man and made the world a better place."

My honest answer would have been "sort of." I had done my best throughout my life. I had been kind and sometimes cruel, generous and sometimes greedy, but I was sure there was more to life than I had discovered. I hadn't yet found the significant thing I was meant to do; therefore I probably hadn't completed whatever mission I was meant to carry out.

Driving home from Wales, I made a deal with God. I was going to help people and do good with my life. I would even book myself on that meditation course the Shiatsu guy had told me about. Finding more peace and joy and living an easier life, would be a good place to start.

Chapter 11. The shark that never was

"The route of all fear is imagination."

– Atsushi Ohkubo, Japanese manga author.

Disasters have a wonderful way of focusing our attention on what truly matters. By shaking us to our core, the details of life are suddenly less important. The gripes, the issues and the negativities fade into the background and we remember what is most important to us. Disasters can be the fastest way to re-prioritise our life, but how long our new priorities last is anybody's guess.

When I was safely back in London, I soon forgot my heartfelt promise on the mountainside. My humility vanished like a magician's rabbit and life once again overtook my good intentions. However, fate wasn't going to let me slither my way out of this one: if I wasn't going to do what I was supposed to do, then I would keep getting reminders. They would keep coming, even if they nearly killed me again.

Later that summer, I drove with my good friends Martin and Jamie to the south coast of England to spend a week in a holiday cottage near Padstow. We were in high spirits, talking about the morning swim across the bay that we were planning to take together.

The swim was about a kilometre and a half and the seawater was far from inviting. Was anyone going to chicken out?

On the first day, the three of us got up early and ambled along the pebbled beach, chatting and teasing each other as good friends do. The sky was overcast and the beach deserted, but our spirits were high.

Swimming in the sea in the UK is not as straight forward as many would believe. There is an unwritten protocol to follow. You must first stand next to the body of water you intend to jump into and scrutinise it with a concerned look on your face. Then follows some pacing up and down as you methodically search for the perfect entry point. Not too rocky, not too deep. Then, a few deep breaths to psyche yourself up, ignoring the memories of private parts leaping towards your armpits to escape the cold. After a couple of false starts, there is no way back, particularly when friends are involved. The wet and the cold must have you. Wimping out, especially in front of good mates is not an option.

Half a minute of shivering later, the freezing cold was replaced by a pleasant, tingling sensation all over my body. I was not sure where my private parts ended up, as I couldn't feel them, but they seemed to survive. It didn't take long for me to warm up, or at least for my body to numb to such a degree that I could no longer feel the cold. This was going well.

"It's fine. It's not that cold," I declared to Martin and Jamie.

I wonder how many seaside holidaymakers regret seeing the movie, Jaws? I certainly did. Whenever I swam in water more than three feet deep, a haunting voice at the back of my mind warned me of an imminent shark attack. Images of the movie flashed into my head and it seemed a gruesome inevitability that a giant fish would appear from nowhere and swallow me whole. I did my best to quell this fear, but when I got into the sea, it appeared, waiting to strike if I gave it half a chance.

"Jaws is a movie," I told myself. *"Great white sharks don't feed off the coast of Cornwall."*

By staying close to my mates, I managed to keep my shark phobia at bay and three quarters of an hour later, we had traversed the murky waters and returned to land, triumphant. The feeling of sitting in front of a log fire in the cottage, wrapped up in warm towels, drinking hot chocolate made it all worthwhile.

The next day we did the same. My confidence was building.

On the third day, the sky was again overcast and the temperature had dropped. As I left the cottage barefoot, wearing only a T-shirt and swimming trunks, I wondered why I was bothering.

"I think I might give it a miss today," I muttered hesitantly.

"Come on. Don't be such a baby," Jamie reassured me sensitively.

"Bollocks,"

I thought, as I picked my way across the sharp barnacles which had welded themselves to the rocks along the shore. I could have gone back to bed and had nothing to do with these foolish antics. Why was I so weak?

My doubts continued as I immersed myself in the sea. Damn it was cold! Jamie and Martin didn't seem to notice.

One thing I hadn't learned at that stage of my life was that the anticipation of an event is usually worse than the event itself. By the time we were a hundred metres from shore, I was once again relishing the whole experience. The waves were choppier and the wind colder, but it felt enlivening to pit myself against nature. I had got this covered.

"You know they've had shark attacks around here," Jamie announced out of nowhere.

"Yeh, I heard that too," added Martin with a

smile.

"I hope there aren't any hungry sharks around. They tend to pick off the weakest swimmers," Jamie continued.

When Jamie said the words "weakest swimmers," he looked straight at me and gave me a grin. I didn't grin back. At university I had studied enough marine biology modules to know the chances of being eaten by a shark were lower than those of meeting Elvis in the supermarket, but my now hyper-stimulated reptilian brain chose to ignore this fact.

"Screw this, I'm going in," I shouted angrily, paddling for the shore.

Martin and Jamie watched, unsure as to whether I meant what I had said or was playing along with their joke. It soon became obvious I wasn't seeing the funny side.

"Chill out!" Jamie shouted after me. "There aren't any sharks. I was having a laugh."

But I wasn't having any of it. My composure had taken off faster than a hungry greyhound out of the traps and I was heading for home as fast as my not-so-impressive swim strokes could carry me. My arms flailed, my legs went bananas and I began to inhale salt water. Then, as is usually the case whenever I panic, it all got an awful lot worse.

The wind picked up and the waves got choppier. Seawater splashed into my face and stung my eyes. What could have been a simple swim for shore became a nightmare. I spluttered and choked and the more I panicked, the tougher it got. My mind was saturated with fear and all I thought about was not making it back to the shore. Some people claim that fear focuses the mind. Fear certainly didn't focus my mind, nor did it improve my swimming strokes. Instead, I made the mistake of trying to swim for the closest part of the shore, straight into the current.

A wise man would have taken his time, swimming at an angle to the tide and keeping his cool. But I was no wise man. I was a stray cat, determined to escape from the great white shark circling below me — a shark, which was bigger than any previously recorded, hadn't eaten for days and had a penchant for small Scottish men.

Cough. Splutter. Choke.

Swallowing salt water isn't pleasant at the best of times, but for a weak swimmer, a hundred metres from the shore, who had convinced himself that the tide was now taking him out to sea, it was murder. Once again, I was in trouble, out of control and at the mercy of the elements. Once again, I had bitten off more than I could chew and began to experience my own mortality. As was now my habit, I began to pray.

"Please God, get me out this. Get me out alive, and I'll do good with my life."

I flailed my way to shore as best I could, with my friends following behind, astonished by this spectacle. After what seemed like half an hour, but was more like ten minutes, I clawed my way up the barnacled rocks on the shore. Furious with Martin and Jamie for getting me into such a state, I stomped back to the cottage in a huff. I was lucky to be alive — no thanks to them.

It didn't take too long for me to see the funny side of their joke. Considering the pranks I had played on them, it was the least I deserved. Despite calling this my second brush with death, I was never close to drowning. I swallowed some seawater and freaked out, but that was about it. What was significant was I thought I might drown. What happens to us is one thing, but how we interpret what happens is everything. This is what forms our perception of reality. In my mind I had been close to death again, which meant my promise to God had been as sincere as it could have been. This time I knew I needed to live my life differently and I needed to do it soon.

Chapter 12. Viva España

"I don't go looking for trouble. Trouble usually finds me."

— Katie McGarry, author.

Neither my Welsh nor Cornish disasters shook me up enough to do anything about changing the way I lived my life and I soon forgot about my seawater spluttered promise. By this stage, you might be wondering if I was missing a few slates from my roof? Surely, I would have got the hint by now?

I regret to say that, back in those days, common sense was not my specialty. Instead of learning to meditate, I thought a better idea would be to go to the Costa del Sol and pick up some of the lingo. Half the world speaks Spanish and I thought it would be a good idea for me to learn too. If you were aware of how my bad my Norwegian sounds after living in Oslo for fifteen years, you would know I needed all the help I could get.

Three weeks later, I was living in Málaga, a few hundred yards from the beach, with a rather gloomy Spanish family. The town was pleasant enough and there were some friendly students at the language school, but I still felt empty. I had transformed my outside world and added some sun, but inside I was the same; agitated and far from peaceful.

My success with the language was even less impressive. I missed half of my lessons and avoided my sinister Spanish family like the plague. Choosing instead to hang out with English-speaking foreigners. My Spanish family were dour, serious people, who seemed allergic to my British sense of humour. Their enthusiasm for visitors, if it had ever existed, had been worn thin by years hosting ungrateful students from all over the world. Once the novelty of the sun, the bars and meeting new people wore off, I didn't feel any closer to happiness. All in all, I was treading water, but slowly sinking.

One Friday evening, a few of us from the language school were devouring paella in a fish restaurant by the sea; speaking English, of course! The evening was hot, but kept pleasantly cool by a steady breeze coming in from the Mediterranean. Fifty yards down the beach, some local lads were tearing up and down the seafront on scooters, pulling wheelies and doing tricks, trying to impress any women unfortunate enough to wander by.

Again and again, they fell off their scooters, picked themselves up, pulled another wheely, then fell over again. This bizarre and clearly painful performance continued, with the lads oblivious to how ridiculous they looked. In that part of Spain, humiliating oneself in the most dramatic way possible to impress the ladies, seemed to be the norm. I guess the subtleties of courtship vary across the globe!

After a few San Miguels and too much paella, my friends and I said good night and headed home. As I walked along the beach with a friend of mine called Kim, three of the scooter guys spotted us and drove over revving their engines. Their intention, no doubt, to impress Kim, who was an attractive American woman.

If you haven't had the pleasure of seeing someone rev a 50cc scooter engine to win the heart of an intelligent young lady, I highly recommend it! It was hilarious. Had I not felt so hostile towards these young men, I would have burst out laughing. Kim wasn't impressed by their antics, but her lack of interest seemed to spur the lads on. They stayed on the beach and continued to squeeze as much noise from their two-wheeled lawnmowers as they could.

Intrigued by this alluring foreigner who wouldn't succumb to their well-hidden charms, they finally got off their bikes and decided to try a more traditional approach, chatting her up. Despite their best efforts to invade Kim's personal space, looking her up and down and making strange whistling sounds, the young men failed to impress her. Can you believe it?

"…whistle, whistle, whistle."

I kept quiet, hoping they would go away. I knew the locals could be over-enthusiastic with their attempts to win a mate for the night and hoped they didn't mean any harm.

"Idiots will be idiots."

But waiting them out didn't work. The leader of the gang, a swarthy, stocky man with curly hair, wouldn't take "no" for an answer. He kept bugging Kim. I found myself in one of those uncomfortable situations where I hoped everything would work out, but feared I might have to be brave.

"…whistle, whistle, whistle."

Enough was enough. This had to stop. A split second before I opened my mouth, I saw myself saying in a calm and commanding voice,
"Come on lads, leave it out, she's not interested."
In those days, diplomacy was not my strong suit and despite my good intentions, slightly different words came out,
"Piss off, you knob, she's not interested," I seethed aggressively. In the spirit of living in Spain,

I said half of this sentence in Spanish — or rather, I tried to. I could have ordered a cheese omelet for all I knew. I don't think the swarthy leader had any idea what I was saying, but understood my tone and his face hardened.

The prospect of fighting this good-for-nothing scoundrel to save a damsel in distress was drawing closer. I've never been much of a tough guy, but at times I used to think I was. Without further ado, I moved towards him, my body ready for the impending violence that would surely unfold. I hoped I would win what would most likely end up as an undignified wrestle on the ground. After all, I was the one defending the damsel. That must count for something?

I took great pride in keeping myself in good shape and had practiced martial arts for many years, but despite my confident demeanor, I did not like violence one little bit.

Sensing my aggression, the scoundrel's two friends stepped forward to support their mate.

"I'll have you lot too," I shouted and now it became three against one. My words sounded hollow, I felt hollow, but I couldn't back down.

I expected the leader to grab or punch me and for the other two to join in, get me on the ground and give me a good kicking.

He didn't.

To my amazement, the swarthy, curly haired man stepped back, flashed me an empty smile and lifted up his sand covered T-shirt. What I saw tucked into his belt stopped me in my tracks. This was not what I had signed up for.

A pistol.

Have you ever had the experience where everything slows down and unfolds in slow motion? You become the watcher, rather than the doer? Well, the next few moments felt like that.

I looked at the gun and then at him. Then at the gun and once again at him. Before or since, I have never seen such an expression of menacing victory in anyone's eyes. My eyes nearly came out of their sockets. Without even throwing a punch, he had smacked me in the guts and I was in no-man's-land.

I felt very, very lost.

What do you do when the guy you're picking a fight with shows you a gun? What do you do when the woman who's standing next to you is relying on you to get her home safely?

Short of bursting into tears and begging for our lives, I had no idea. So, I did nothing, except put my arm around Kim and whisper,

"Oh."

Then Kim whispered,

"Oh."

Then the guy with the gun also whispered,

"Oh."

Then, without another word, he and his friends turned around, jumped on their scooters and rode away into the night.

Chapter 13. Business as usual

"Life is a fight, but not everyone's a fighter. Otherwise, bullies would be an endangered species.

– Andrew Vachss, author and attorney.

Despite the previous night's lucky escape, nothing had changed — except I had another good story to tell. Instead of taking time to reflect on yet another near miss, I spent the morning boasting about my bravery to my friends. The gods must have been looking down on me and shaking their heads in dismay. Was I ever going to take the hint?

That evening, I had another truly inspired idea. Why not go out in Malaga alone and have a few too many beers?

Drinking wasn't good for me. I was one of those guys who got drunk, started believing I was God's gift to women, tried to convince them of this fact, failed, and then stormed home in a huff feeling sorry for myself. Goodness knows why I bothered, but idiots will be idiots and my inflated ego still ruled my life with an iron rod.

A few beers and a couple of failed chat-up attempts later, I found myself walking home on my own. I was so engulfed in self pity, I didn't notice I was hopelessly lost until I found myself heading out of town on a road I didn't recognise.

"Damn it!"

I thought and stuck out my hand to hail a taxi. The moment I did, three scooters shot passed with two guys on each one. They were young guys; macho guys, just like the guys from the night before and I had caught their attention. The taxi drove on without stopping and the scooters pulled to a halt in front of me.

"Oh no, not again."

In seconds I had sobered up, then looked around to see if I could spot an escape route. To my right was an unlit beach and to my left were deserted office buildings. My biggest problem was that nobody was around. It was just me, the occasional passing car and the scooter guys. I couldn't have found a lonelier place to meet trouble. The scooter guys turned their bikes around and pulled up beside me.

"Hey, you are missing? What's up man?" one

of them asked me in broken English, as he looked me up and down.

"I'm just going for a walk. Dondé the taxi rank is?" I replied, in equally broken Spanish, hoping they might take pity on a lost foreigner taking a late night stroll.

"Si, eez on the beach. Come with us," another answered sarcastically.

No way was I was going to follow these guys onto the beach. If I was lucky, they would only take my wallet, but I smelled violence and I don't think I would have escaped without a good hiding. I turned away from them and continued to walk up the road, but they didn't take the hint. The whole gang rode after me, taking great joy in buzzing around me on their scooters before scootering away. Trouble was brewing, but I couldn't figure out how to avoid it.

Every so often, they would all ride off and just as I thought they had lost interest, they would turn around and cruise past me again. This sick game of cat and mouse went on for half an hour and I had no idea what to do. As time went on, fewer and fewer cars drove past, my options were shrinking.

After twenty minutes, they finally sped off for good, in search of another form of mindless entertainment to keep themselves amused. As the noise of their engines faded into the distance, then fell silent, I breathed a long sigh of relief.

"That was close."

Five minutes later, they reappeared. Now I knew I was running out of time. If a taxi didn't come along soon, I would have to face them — all six of them. I didn't fancy my chances.

The gang pulled up ahead of me for one last time and turned off their engines. The silence that remained was anything but golden.

"Oh, no."

Time had run out. Something had to give. I took a deep breath and walked straight up to the gang, praying they wouldn't mug me — or worse. I will never forget that experience: six guys, some standing, some sitting on their scooters, all staring me down. But I had a chance. It was slim, but it was there. Behind the gang was a dark alleyway and at the end of that alleyway I could see a taxi rank in the distance. I didn't know what taxi rank was in Spanish, but in English it spelled "freedom" If I could look each of the scooter gang in the eyes and bluff my way past them, perhaps they would leave me alone?

Acting as calmly as I could, with my heart racing and adrenaline pumping, I began to walk past each of them in turn, unconsciously holding my breath. I passed two of them and all was well. Then I passed the third; a tall, thin youth with a cigarette tucked behind his ear. Then numbers four and five who didn't hold my gaze. So far none of them had so much as lifted a finger. Perhaps they were just trying to unnerve a foreigner for sport?

As I approached the last guy, he grabbed the arm of my leather jacket. That was a big mistake. I had been given that jacket by an old friend and it meant a great deal to me. The jacket was made from soft black leather; one of the remnants of my trading days. Never would I let it fall into the hands of some scumbag, no matter what price I had to pay.

"Good jacket," the scumbag said.

I scowled and shoved him in the chest, putting some weight behind it. He stumbled backwards, let go of my jacket, but did nothing else.

"Phew," I thought. *"I guess they're not as tough as they look."*

As I walked on, a surge of relief swept through me. I was unharmed and still in possession of my wallet and jacket. What was it with me and guys on scooters?

I didn't hear the two sets of footsteps approaching from behind until it was too late. Before I could turn around, one of the gang grabbed me around my neck, pulling me backwards onto the pavement. Another swung a punch at my head but missed.

I couldn't believe it. How could they be so cowardly as to jump me from behind?

"What the…?"

These pricks had hassled me for half an hour

and only had the guts to finish the job when my back was turned. I was furious and to make matters worse they had scuffed the arm of my leather jacket. I snapped and a rage far beyond anything I had ever known, possessed me. Leaping to my feet, I pointed at the nearest one and yelled,

"Right. I'm going to have you. I'm going to have all of you."

The power of my voice filled me with confidence, as if a giant was standing behind me screaming at them. They didn't expect such ferocity from a little guy and for a moment I had the upper hand. The band of cowards sprinted away, but before they could escape, I ran forward and punched the nearest one in the face as hard as I could. It felt great to land the punch, but it wasn't a good one. I caught him on his cheek bone; one of the hardest parts of the body and not a good place to punch anyone if you want to hurt them. But I did a good job of bruising my hand.

I had no intention of stopping there and ran towards the rest of them seeking vengeance. I must have looked like a madman chasing them down the street, screaming blue murder. I was so caught up in the rage, it didn't occur to me to escape down the dark alley to the safety of the taxi rank. Instead, I pursued them, intent on teaching them a lesson they would never forget.

Chapter 14. Finally!

"Your unhappiness ultimately arises not from the circumstances of your life but from the conditioning of your mind."

– Eckhart Tolle, spiritual teacher.

Sprinting towards the gang, it dawned on me that if I kept after them, I was going to get myself into deep water. As quickly as my courage had arrived, it could drain from my bones and I would be left vulnerable and outnumbered. The gang hadn't seen that I was half-drunk, but they soon would. Cutting my losses, I jogged to a halt, spun around and ran in the opposite direction, disappearing into the darkness of the unlit alley as fast as my legs would carry me.

o   o   o

An hour later I was lying in bed, staring at the

ceiling, wondering if I had woken up my doleful Spanish family by crashing into my room at three o'clock in the morning? My thoughts drifted to my near miss with the scooter gang and then to the pistol episode on the beach with Kim. Two close shaves in two nights, I had been lucky to escape serious injury or worse. Then my thoughts drifted to Cornwall and my not-so-near-death "shark" encounter. I smiled as I remembered what a fuss I had made over one small comment. Finally, I felt the terror of being trapped on a Welsh mountainside with Matt. Closing my eyes, I relived these events in my mind, wondering if they had any significance. Was it pure coincidence I had experienced so much drama in the last few months? My life had had its ups and downs, but this was getting out of hand. I wracked my brain to find an answer, but none came.

My knuckles hurt, I was probably going to be thrown out of my lodgings and a stinking hangover was waiting for me. In this turbulent state a truly remarkable thing happened. As I lay on my back, aware of my chest rising and falling, I stopped fighting with my thoughts. I don't know how this happened. Whether I did something different or the fighting stopped for no apparent reason.

In the space of a short second, I gave up trying to understand why any of these unusual events had occurred. Lying on a lumpy bed in Malaga, staring into the blackness beyond my mind, my internal struggle stopped and a deep peace emerged from within. Back in those days, peace wasn't on my list of everyday experiences. I was so used to being a slave to my non-stop mind, I didn't know there was any other way to experience life, other than through the chaos of my addled thoughts. When the peace arrived it deeply affected me.

"Wow!"

It felt incredible.

Trying to describe it doesn't do it justice, but it was some kind of silent, unmoving presence that was soft and full of love. It stretched forever, holding everything in it, in the way outer space holds planets in it. I had never felt anything like this stillness before, yet it was somehow familiar. Here I was, a thousand miles from Scotland, living with the Spanish equivalent of the Addams family, but I felt at home. All my thoughts and worries quickly left, dwarfed by this peaceful presence. I felt free, without problems or stress. No longer thinking about the challenges I had faced, or the problems that lay ahead of me. No longer thinking about anything at all. I could have happily stayed in this state forever.

Then it came to me. Not from the lateral, logical, thinking part of my mind, but as a spark of intuition that presented itself and then disappeared. These dramas weren't isolated coincidences; they had been trying to give me a message. Life had been doing its best to tell me something and when I hadn't listened, it had smacked me over the head, four times. Life was trying to tell me I was going in the wrong direction. It didn't have anything against me, it had no desire to punish me, but it *had* to get my attention. Those four experiences were tough love. I had known for years I wanted to find peace, but I hadn't done what was required. I had been trying to find it by making money so I could change my life, yet here it was, perfect happiness engulfing me in a lumpy bed in Spain.

The chaos in my life had accelerated after my encounter with the shiatsu healer in Edinburgh. Only days after I had prayed for help on Wimbledon Common, he had told me I needed to learn to ascend. He said it would make me wiser and wisdom was a quality that was distinctly lacking in my life. But I had ignored his words. It didn't take a genius to conclude that perhaps this ancient form of meditation was part of the puzzle? If I could learn to ascend, I could find more peace and joy and live an easier life.

That was it! I needed to learn to ascend.

I needed to fly back to England and find out if this meditation was the real deal and it didn't seem like I had a choice. I had to do it.

The next day, I packed in my disastrous Spanish course, said farewell to my friends at the language school, grumbled adios to my dolorous Spanish family and flew back to London.

Sitting on the plane as it took off from Malaga airport, I looked out of the window and remembered the optimism I had felt when flying out of New York. This time I didn't let myself feel optimistic, but I did feel sure I was doing the right thing. At last, I had made a good, balanced decision that might take me somewhere. In one way I felt I had more control over my life and in another I felt I had none.

By a stroke of luck, an Ishayas' Ascension as taught by the Brightpath course was scheduled a few days later in the small town of Glastonbury in the West Country. I rang up the course organiser and booked myself in.

Chapter 15. The course

"Have you ever noticed that anybody driving slower than you is an idiot, and anyone going faster than you is a maniac?"

– George Carlin, comedian.

Sitting in the carriage of the westbound train, I wondered what I was getting myself into. Meditation was a hippy thing, wasn't it?

Would the other participants on the course be a gaggle of dreadlocked, cardigan-wearing, dope-smoking dropouts, moaning about big business and the state of the planet? I hoped not. I had lived with a group of hippies in Australia, who had been lovely people, but I had offended them by cooking up steaks and sausages, when all they ate was lentils and green beans.

Then another thought struck me.

"How on earth am I going to meditate for a whole

weekend?"

I found it hard to sit through an episode of EastEnders.

Beverley, the course organiser, picked me up at Castle Cary railway station in a bright yellow mini. She was a lively, forty-year-old with striking black hair that exploded from her scalp in untamable curls. The first thing I noticed about her was her smile, it was genuine and came easily. Beverley seemed normal enough until she got onto the open road, where she revealed a taste for speed which was unnerving to say the least.

Hurtling along the country roads at close to Mach 3, I sat glued to my seat, my feet jammed hard onto the footrests and my thighs twitching every time she slammed on the brakes.

"Can you tell me about the course or is it a secret?" I asked Beverley, more to keep my attention off her driving than to make polite conversation.

"Sure. It's called the First Sphere," she replied, looking directly at me for longer than was safe. Her voice was soft, considering her car was on two wheels at the time.

"Have you found peace?" I asked her through gritted teeth.

"Mmm. Well, I'm happier than I was before I learned. I wouldn't say I've found peace, as you can see by my driving" — she grinned, giving me a wink — "but life is easier. I'm more relaxed and creative. I feel more like me."

"But how do you quiet your mind? I can't stop my thoughts," I asked, hoping I would survive long enough to learn to ascend.

"Me neither," she replied, "you don't need to quiet your mind. Thoughts are fine. It's easier to find peace if you're not fighting with your thoughts."

It seemed to make sense.

Beverley squinted her eyes, assessing whether to overtake a tractor on the blind corner we were fast approaching. I looked at the hedgerows shooting past, had we been driving a little slower I might have admired them. Right now, they were no more than a blur. Beverley didn't seem the type who could slow down even if I asked her to, so I didn't

"Who's teaching the course?"

"Two Ishaya monks."

"Monks? What would they be like? Would they have long brown cassocks and bald heads? Perhaps a Bible or two knocking around?"

I smiled as images of the irate Presbyterian minister from my childhood returned to me.

"I hope they're more relaxed than he was."

"Is this some sort of religious thing?" I asked.

"No — it's about experiencing rather than believing. There's more to it than meets the eye." Beverley's bumper passed within inches of the tractor. "Wow!" she gasped. "Sorry about that."

We got to Beverley's home in one piece and as I carried my rucksack towards the front door, I met the first of the two Ishaya monks. Taking up the whole doorway, like some grizzly bear blocking the sun, was Samadeva.

"Samadeva. Pleased to meet ya," he beamed, as he offered me an enormous paw. I took to him instantly. It was hard not to like someone with a smile that big. The other Ishaya, a fine-featured woman, emerged from behind Samadeva with a cup of coffee in her hand. She introduced herself as Rodavi. Rodavi was shy, almost feline in the way she moved, but had a pleasant, peaceful feel about her.

Over the weekend I learned that these monks were not how I had pictured monks. They didn't wear brown cassocks; they weren't affiliated to any religious order and the rules they followed were ones which guided them and others towards more peace and happiness. They weren't hidden away in a secluded monastery, instead they chose to live their lives in the hustle and bustle of the modern world. Modern-day meditating monks was the catchiest way I could describe them and they made a deep impression on me.

Despite their strange names, they weren't pretentious at all. Samadeva, judging by the size of him and his enthusiasm at mealtimes, liked the good life. He was from America, an ex-GI soldier who had quit the army and gone searching for meaning. He had some great stories and still possessed the energy of an upbeat, ready to help, soldier. Rodavi was the more mysterious of the pair, dressing only in black and not talking unless she deemed it necessary. She was not someone who smiled much, but seemed happy none-the-less. She was also American and drank black coffee like it was going out of fashion.

Whenever I chatted to Samadeva, I couldn't help but enjoy the big guy's company. I liked sitting near him, even when we weren't talking. For the first time in my life, I didn't feel I needed to make conversation with another person in the room. I couldn't put my finger on it, but he had an x-factor I wanted, a kind of depth.

A young woman, presumably another participant, walked into the room and introduced herself as Mars.

"Oh my God!" I thought. *"Not another weird name."*

Mars was dressed in a green sweater with a rainbow-coloured beanie over her dreadlocked head. She was a singer from Australia and despite my reservations about hippies, I liked her. That she had beautiful eyes and sang like an angel helped too.

Sitting on a comfy sofa in a cosy sitting room in Glastonbury, on the first evening of the First Sphere course, I enjoyed listening to the two monks talk. To hear people who were at peace talk about peace was a pleasure. Their words made me

113

peaceful too.

When it came to meditating, or ascending as they called it, things weren't what I expected. The moment I closed my eyes, a barrage of thoughts entered my mind. I have no idea what I thought about, but I was all over the place.

After a few minutes, Samadeva told us to open our eyes and I breathed a sigh of relief.

"How was it?" he asked innocently.

I paused for a moment.

"Well, I had hundreds of thoughts and it felt like we were ascending for a very long time," I told him, feeling guilty for moaning. "All I had wanted was to open my eyes and go and do something, anything to take my mind off the boredom."

Samadeva listened intently and then turned to Mars. Had I made a mistake coming on the course?

"That was amazing!" proclaimed Mars in her Melbourne twang. "I saw a bright, golden light appear over my crown chakra. Then someone — it sounded like an angel — started to sing to me. The song was the most beautiful I've ever heard. Real magical. It's given me a great idea for a new song."

A solitary, spiritual tear rolled down Mars' cheek as she shared her profound experience. I shrank into the sofa, pretending I wasn't there. How come the hippy was such an expert and I just had loads of thoughts?

"Damn it."

"It's normal to have thoughts when you ascend, Ollie. It's also fine to fee bored, particularly if you've been a bit stressed out. Don't worry about it — it'll get easier," Samadeva reassured me. Then uttered the words which had been following me around since I met the Shiatsu healer: "Hang in there. If you do this, you'll find more peace and joy."

What choice did I have? I was stuck in the depths of Somerset for the weekend and had been through a lot to get here. I wasn't going to let a bit of boredom and a few million thoughts stop me. Some people want a quick fix. A fix which doesn't involve much commitment. They want so much but aren't prepared to sacrifice anything to get it. I can understand this approach because I was impatient too. If I could have swallowed a pill which would have given me endless peace, I would have jumped at the chance. However, to achieve anything worthwhile, I knew I had to put in the hours. Besides, I wasn't a wimp, I liked a challenge.

As the course went on, Mars continued to tell us about her mind-blowing experiences, which became more impressive each time we ascended. My experience stayed the same; boring, restless and thought filled. Every time Mars spoke, I rolled my eyes, but I couldn't help being fascinated by her outlandish experiences.

o   o   o

In Glastonbury, there is a grassy hill, known as the Tor, which overlooks the ancient town. On top of the Tor stands an old, stone tower, built as a beacon for travellers who approached from all directions. Beverley's house wasn't far from the Tor and after lunch I decided to walk there, alone.

Standing on top of the Tor, taking in the higgledy piggledy rooftops of the shops and houses below, I noticed the world looked different. A wizened old tree, which wouldn't typically have caught my eye, drew my attention. The tree was so beautiful and alive, every branch and knot perfect and enchanting. I cast my gaze towards the hedges and the fields below. Sheaves of barley swayed in harmony and I could have sworn nature herself was more beautiful than she had ever been.

"Wow!"

I had grown up in the countryside in the Highlands of Scotland. A wild and picturesque place where nature was always close at hand. Whilst it had been a stunning place to live, I had taken its beauty for granted. A tree was a tree. A field a field. Well, now it wasn't, the tree was colourful, alive and to be appreciated. This experience was different to the euphoric manias I had gone through with bipolar. It was grounded and I didn't get carried away with the soft emotions of appreciation I felt. I stood on the Tor for the best part of an hour, looking out across this new world feeling deeply peaceful and happy.

The countryside was the same as it had been the day before, but I was seeing it differently. After two days of ascending, was I starting to see the world through new eyes?

That experience spurred me on. What was a little boredom compared to this?

Chapter 16. The Presence within

"The primary cause of unhappiness is never the situation but your thoughts about it."

– Eckhart Tolle, spiritual teacher.

Fortunately, those boring, thought filled ascensions didn't last forever and my racing mind, which used to cause me so many problems, began to calm down. At the same time, I noticed a presence within me, which I could describe as a kind of nothingness or space. This presence was still, tangible and unmoving. I couldn't see it, but I could experience it.

When I first began ascending, it only appeared when I was meditating in a group. After some months, it began to show itself when I was ascending alone. It felt like the peace I had experienced in my bed in Spain and the radiant

118

awareness I had found whilst parachuting, but not as intense. I can best describe it as a quiet, inner stillness that felt like home. It was not a feeling I was used to, but one I wanted to become better acquainted with.

For long periods in my life, I had been wearing an invisible suit of armour. I had presented an "I've got it together" image, but the truth was far from it. I was good at acting as if I had it all together, but inside I was often insecure, afraid or frustrated. Now I was taking off the armour, piece by piece.

As the armour fell away, the presence entered my life. Initially, I only experienced it with my eyes shut in meditation, usually towards the end of an ascension session. However, after a few months it began to appear when I was going about my business with my eyes open. I would be walking in the woods and sense this presence within me. I would be watching television and feel it.

Being able to ascend with my eyes open as well as closed, enabled this presence to find its way into my everyday life. My eyes closed practice helped me to relax and destress my nervous system and ascending with my eyes open reduced the amount of stress that built up in me. The practice was so simple that I could walk down the street ascending and even do it in a traffic jam. So, I did it every day.

o   o   o

The presence is a state which is unaffected by worries, stress or anxiety. A state where I felt free from the troubles of my mind. Negative thoughts could float by, but if I was present, they didn't affect me. The presence reminded me of those times in my life when I had felt at my most happy and safe. I had experienced that state often as a child, but as I grew up, I had forgotten about it. That is one of the most perverse parts of growing up. Developing from being a happy child to becoming a serious, worldly burdened adult. I had done it, as had everyone else I knew. However, now I was reversing the process. Strangely, this simple presence revealed itself as the key to experiencing what I truly wanted, lasting happiness and peace.

It seemed the more I tapped into it, the richer my experience of life became — not necessarily in obvious ways, like being showered with gifts or getting exactly what I wanted, but in deeper, subtler ways. The magic of being alive became obvious. Praise, gratitude, love and compassion became more common place, in myself and others. I became more sensitive to situations and more in tune with myself. A confidence deeper than the "go get 'em" false confidence I had relied on for much of my life revealed itself. I was remembering who I really was! I was no longer some guy struggling to make it in the world, but a content, alive man who wasn't too shaken by the ups and downs of life.

After a few months, I discovered I didn't have

to cross my fingers and wait for it to arrive. I could choose to experience the presence whenever I wanted, merely by choosing to experience it. After that, the presence began to accompany me throughout the day. I had learned how to make a very important choice, a choice that connected me to the flow of life. My soul was getting a warm bath.

I had previously associated London with stress and problems, but now I was able to find peace amongst the shoppers and commuters on a Friday afternoon in rush hour!

Presence is a simple state, which many of us drop into it from time to time, when we are driving or performing simple tasks which require no thinking. Instead of figuring out what to do, we just do. Athletes call it "the zone." Getting acquainted with it, diving into it, and uniting with it is a real adventure.

Does being able to reach this state make me superhuman? Can I fly? Can I read people's minds and levitate?

Nope.

I'm an ordinary man who lives a fairly ordinary life. Yet I am more peaceful than I ever thought I would be. I find such pleasure in the simple things. The presence continues to grow and with it my ease and enjoyment of life. It doesn't mean that my life is always a success or that I don't face challenges. I do. What it means is that I am better equipped to deal with those challenges.

When I learned to ascend, I wasn't a

particularly happy guy. Working at the bank had taken its toll and I wasn't coping well with the external pressures of life or the internal pressures of my own mental programming, but over time I began to feel different. Ascension showed me the different voices in my head, which had ruled over me for the best part of my life. Once I saw them, they began to lose their power. They became thoughts, rather than reality. My judgments fell away and the world I saw was a better place. People were friendlier and many of my relationships richer. I even stopped being afraid of horses and sharks!

When I was fearful, I saw a scary world. When I was at peace, I saw a friendlier world. It was the same world, but I experienced it differently, depending on my emotional state. I had been wearing dark glasses, which made the world appear far darker than it was. Now I had taken those glasses off and what I saw was brighter. For the first time, I knew that everything was okay. I was okay.

In general, young children experience presence more readily than adults who tend to overthink their lives. They don't regret the past or worry about the future, they just experience life as it is right now. I started out the same way, but as I grew older, my relationship with my mind changed and I started to think more. I got into the habit of thinking all day long and I lost my connection with the happy, non-thinking me. I was grabbed by whatever thoughts were passing through my mind and consumed by them. The presence began to change my relationship with these thoughts. It allowed me to observe them, rather than be consumed by them.

The growth that occurs on a spiritual path is rarely linear. There are periods of so called "stability" where nothing seems to happen, followed by a leaps forward in consciousness. Patience is required, as the leaps are exciting when they happen, but never constant.

Some time after I had learned to ascend, something dramatic happened to me. I woke up one morning and my thoughts had moved from buzzing around the space between my ears, to being further away from me. They had been loud and were now far quieter. From that moment on, they began to live in the background of my mind and for the most part have stayed there ever since. Replacing their presence was presence. Gosh, it felt peaceful.

As the years went on, my need to drive myself to be successful diminished. Many of my strong desires, which were often built around proving myself and negating my low self-worth, evaporated. This allowed a feeling of contentment to creep into my life and I became more grateful for what I had. I still like to have goals, I think they make life more interesting, but I do not chase them with an unhealthy intensity and am at peace whether they are fulfilled or not. There is great freedom in not needing to be a success to be happy.

I had one panic attack a few weeks after the course in Glastonbury and since then I have not had another. That is twenty years without one.

As far as my path to peace has been concerned, bipolar has thrown a few spanners in the works. The peace I have found through Ascension has helped me a great deal, but it isn't of any use when I am deeply depressed, manic, or psychotic. Only my family's love, medication and professional support seem to help me during the worst episodes. However, for the long periods when I have been mentally stable, Ascension has allowed me to be happier than I had previously imagined. It has also enabled me to spot the early warning signs of an episode, so I can do something about it before it consumes me.

At times I have been disheartened, especially when I was going through tough times with bipolar or my personal life. It would have been easy for me to give up ascending, but fortunately I knew what I wanted. I wanted freedom from emotional suffering and I believed Ascension would help me find that if I persisted. So, I did. I kept going.

I stumbled upon what I believe most people are looking for: a spiritual path which has led me to lasting inner peace. I am not sure how I found a path that so suited me. Perhaps I had accrued good karma in some other lifetime? Or perhaps I was so desperately lost and my desire for peace so strong, I was prepared to do anything to get it? Whatever the reason, I discovered what most people want more than anything and this short book is my way of sharing that.

It is a bold statement to claim I know what you want and it is not meant to sound conceited. I could be wrong. You might want a Ferrari, financial freedom or good health more than anything. You might want happiness for your family or even the whole world. But the chances are, if you get any of these, they will give you a feeling of happiness and peace. So, perhaps what you really want is peace? Perhaps underneath our material desires is the desire for an inner state?

I do not believe that everyone should learn Ascension. It has been a fast and direct path for me, but it is not for everyone. What I do believe is that anyone who really wants to experience peace, to be free of emotional suffering and the vagaries of the fickle mind, would be wise to find something that leads them to presence and helps them cultivate that experience.

Chapter 17. Conclusion

"I am the master of my fate, I am the captain of my soul."
– William Ernest Henley, poet.

People influence each other in a variety of ways and by finding peace, I believe we make the world a more peaceful place. When I hang out with angry people, I'm more likely to be angry or afraid. When I hang out with happy people, the chances are I feel happier and more positive about life. Because the presence leads to a growth in happiness, which is itself contagious, it contributes positively to the lives of the people around us. A kind, peaceful, generous person is a bonus in almost any family or group. The idea that I am contributing positively to society by cultivating presence in myself has motivated me to continue ascending for over twenty years.

All the success in the world means little if we

wake up feeling disgruntled every morning. No matter who you are, if you are not at peace, then the gift of life cannot be fully appreciated. With thousands of thoughts rushing around our head, fully enjoying life is impossible. We can do quite well, but ultimately, we end up suffering. True happiness is found within us. It is available whether we are on the beach or in a board meeting. Whether we are rich or poor. Finding true happiness isn't about rearranging our lives; it is about cultivating an ongoing experience of presence, which changes our relationship with our thoughts and emotions.

A state of peace and presence exists inside everyone, waiting to be discovered. There's no one too stupid or too clever, too good or too bad to find it. Freedom, happiness and life are waiting for anyone who genuinely desires to find them and has the courage to do something about it…

Do you have the courage?

Epilogue

Once I had been ascending for a year, I felt the pull to go on a six-month retreat in the mountains of British Columbia, Canada. What I found on the retreat was what I had been looking for. A group of people dedicated to peace and a spiritual path and Teacher who could help me move towards that goal.

I made some good friends and learned much about my mind, the presence, spiritual growth and helping others. It was on that retreat that my desire to dedicate my life to inner peace was solidified.

It has been nearly twenty years since I took that leap of faith and became an Ishaya monk and I am still going. I was given the name Maitreya by my Teacher. Maitreya means The Friendly God. Now, most people know me as Maitreya.

After a few years of teaching all over the world, I spent nearly two years on a retreat centre in the jungle in Mexico. It was a wild, romantic five-hundred-year-old Hacienda, which had only been fitted with electricity the year before. It been built by the Conquistadors and still held some of the magic of that time. It was here that I met the woman who was to become my wife, Hiranya.

A whirlwind romance followed and I moved to Oslo, where I have lived for the last seventeen years.

Much of my time in Oslo has been spent working as a life coach (specialising in mental health), teaching Ascension, giving talks and writing books. I have had my challenges with bipolar, which are better described in my book, Befriending Bipolar: a patient's perspective, but over the years my life has become more and more meaningful. I now live a simpler life than I did as a sales trader, with very different priorities, but I enjoy it very much and am curious as to what it will bring.

Oliver's other book

Befriending Bipolar: a patient's perspective

What is it like to be overtaken by mental illness and completely lose yourself in madness? With staggering insight and brutal honesty, Oliver Seligman describes what insanity is like from the inside.

Diagnosed with type one bipolar at seventeen. Oliver has battled with euphoric manias, suicidal depressions, bewildering psychoses and the side effects of psychiatric medication.

In this enlightening book, he writes about how he found peace with an illness that destroys lives and sometimes ends them. Sharing what worked and what didn't work for him, as well as the mistakes he made and traps he fell into. If you want to learn more about bipolar or depression from someone who has experienced it, this book is for you.

Befriending Bipolar: a patient's perspective is available on Amazon in Kindle and paperback versions.

THANK YOU

Thank you for reading this book. If you enjoyed it, please leave a review on Amazon.
I read every review and they help new readers discover my book.

If you are interested in hiring Oliver as a speaker, meditation teacher or coach please email him on: oliverseligman@gmail.com:

To find out more about The Ishayas' Ascension as taught by the Brightpath, please check out:

www.thebrightpath.com

THANK YOU AGAIN

Hiranya for all your love, support and companionship.

Priya and Hiranya for the brilliant book cover.

My parents for their love and patience.

Lukas, for your passion and pure heart.

Meera and Caroline for great editing.

Thanks also to Charlie, Garuda, Govinda, Paramananda, Devadatta, Sri, Suvarna, Shanti, Maharani, Pavitra, Narain, Matt, Mike, Jim and Rex.

Printed in Great Britain
by Amazon